MISSION RESOURCE NETWORK

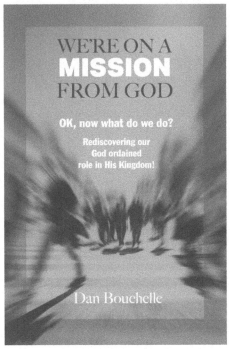

WE'RE ON A
MISSION
FROM GOD

OK, now what do we do?

Rediscovering our
God ordained
role in His Kingdom!

Dan Bouchelle

All proceeds from the sale of this book will be donated to MRN. You may also wish to donate to MRN via the following website link.

www.mrnet.org

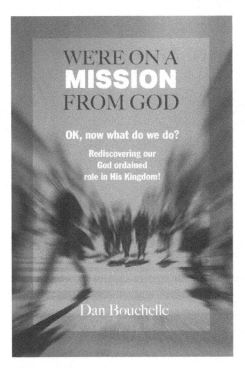

We're on a
Mission from God

Ok, now what do we do?
Rediscovering our God ordained role in his
Kingdom!

Dan Bouchelle

HCU Media LLC
Accra, Ghana ◆ Frisco, TX

We're on a Mission from God

Published and Copyright © 2021
By Dan Bouchelle & HCU Media LLC

ISBN-13: 978-1-939468-19-2 (Paperback Edition)

Also available in Kindle Format (978-1-939468-20-8)

Scripture quotations, unless otherwise noted, are from The Holy Bible, Revised Standard Version, copyright 1971, Zondervan Bible Publishers.

Cover Design by Dale Henry - www.dalehenrydesign.com

First Edition November 2021
10 9 8 7 6 5 4 3 2

Praise for We're on a Mission from God

After over two decades in domestic ministry and over a decade in global missions, Dan Bouchelle offers what he has learned from the global church and missiologists to address the challenges being faced by the American church and churches shaped around the world by America missionaries.

Here are reactions from readers of *We're on a Mission from God*.

Mike Cope – Pepperdine University – Director of Ministry Outreach and Preaching Minister for over 35 years.

What does it mean for the church to be "missional"? The answer to that is critical, and Bouchelle is a trusted guide with this sweeping look at the story of God in scripture — from creation and the calling of Abraham to the death and resurrection of Jesus on to the consummation of God's new creation. This book needs to be put in the hands of church leaders everywhere to help refocus on the calling, identity, and mission of the church. Even though he boldly confronts some of our false gods that have distracted us, I find this book to be deeply hopeful!

Evertt Huffard – Missionary, former Dean of Harding School of Theology, consultant, and preacher.

If you ever dreamed of visiting churches outside the USA to discover what God is doing, you will enjoy reading this book by someone who has done just that. This book will raise your horizon for the mission of the church, clarify the blessing of the Gospel, and challenge what you might think the church needs to do in response to our changing world. These reflections effectively weave theology, the Word, and praxis into a compelling appeal for the church to be on mission as a kingdom that is not of this world. Adapting a famous quote of Mark Twain from *Innocents Abroad*: "Travel is fatal to prejudice . . . and narrow mindedness . . ." -- a perspective of the global church can be fatal to our purposeless, consumer driven, fear and reactivity. The hope of any church will always be found in the fulfillment of the mission of God. This book can help adjust the trajectory of any church to fulfill a divine calling.

Grady King – Leader – Hope Network and Preaching Minister for over 40 years

Every believer in Christ needs to read this concise, biblically robust, and provocative work. Bouchelle's practical understanding of God's mission is refreshing for congregational leaders seeking God's guidance as they address contemporary culture and how believers can reclaim God's mission. You will be blessed, challenged, and maybe even irritated as he identifies how we have abandoned or lost our grip on God's mission. But you will not miss the clarion call to shift from saving our institutions to participating in God's mission. The time is now. The gospel is GOOD NEWS!

Sean Palmer – Teaching Pastor Eccleisa Houston, author & consultant

Hardly anyone knows what to do about mission anymore. Some American Christians no longer care, choosing to busy themselves with faux threats. Others remain committed to missionary methods which today can look like colonial exports of western cultural expectations and preferences. And still there are others who throw up their hands, figuring God will sort it all out. Dan Bouchelle helps us navigate all these rocks and shoals, and much more. His is a needed voice for God's church and God's mission in a time a great confusion. _We're On a Mission from God_, and Dan helps us reclaim the fullness of it.

Luke Norsworthy – Senior Minister of Westover Church of Christ and popular podcast host of "Norsworthy"

I bet you are like many of us who want to be a part of God's renewal of all things, but don't know where to start. Dan Bouchelle will both help you understand what the good news is and show how to share it right where you are. To restore the Church, we must rediscover our mission. This book will be great first step in that restoration.

Jeff Hubbard – Preaching Minister – North Davis Church of Christ:

We're on a Mission from God is a great reminder that the 'mission' God invites us on is not a one time or far off endeavor but an adventure we are on everyday wherever we go. As Christians we are not lawyers, teachers, or doctors, instead we are 'missionaries' in courtrooms, classrooms, and operating rooms. Dan's reminder to not lose sight of the 'mission of God', is an important nudge to returning to the Kingdom people we were created to be.

Brock Paulk - Senior Minister - Heritage Church of Christ:

We're on a Mission from God speaks a word of clarity in a cultural and historic moment when the church may be tempted to turn inward rather than follow God forward. Dan Bouchelle invites the church to bravely look past temporary, earthly distractions, and refocus on the grand story of God's mission to redeem and restore the world. This book will propel our conversations forward in the direction God calls us to go.

Acknowledgements and Thanks

Just as it takes a village to raise a child, no book is the product of any individual. There is no way to give proper credit to everyone who has contributed to this book, which is in many ways a compilation of everything I have learned in my walk with Jesus over 55 years of life and 34 years of ministry. I grew up in a minister's family, with a deep respect for my parents who were my first teachers. My parents have been lifelong learners who have continued to grow into their senior years. They still love to read and learn from what others are saying and doing.

The church has been the majority context of my entire life. I couldn't name all my teachers in the church, nor could I recall the names of all my teachers at the various schools I've attended in preparation for ministry. Then there are all the authors and speakers whose work has shaped me. I worry I've plagiarized the thoughts of others and just don't know it. The risk factor is high. But one of my core beliefs is that there is no intellectual property in the Kingdom of God. If it is of the Lord, we can't claim it. If it isn't, may it be forgotten. Still, it is important to honor those whom the Lord has used to shape us.

Toward that end, I want to thank Leonard Allen, who has been one of my most formative teachers, friends, conversation partners, and a perennial inspiration for over 30 years. He is the one who read the earliest form of this material, when it was a Bible Class curriculum, and suggested that if I reformatted it and edited it, it could serve others well as a book. He read multiple versions of this manuscript and has improved it considerably. I also wish to thank Jack Reece, another important teacher who turned into a dear friend, who got me involved in the missional church conversation many years ago and has made significant contributions to this work, both in the shaping of my thinking for many years and his review of an earlier form of this book. I owe a debt to the Central Church of Christ in Amarillo, Texas, especially the elders, who allowed me to experiment with transitioning that century old downtown congregation toward a more missional expression of church when I had no experience doing something of that nature. The church for whom I created the Bible Class curriculum which became this book was the Central Church who asked me to come back and share with them what I had learned from my work with the global church at MRN.

I also owe a massive debt to the trustees and my co-workers at Mission Resource Network who have been my conversation partners and teachers in living out the mission of God in creative and dynamic ways all around the planet. Because of relationships with global leaders which were built mostly by others, I have been able to learn from the global church and from my co-workers who have well over a century of combined missions experience. Much of what you read here was developed within this community which has been engaged in global missions together as a spiritual community as well as a team of co-workers.

I wish to thank Rick Atchley and The Hills church. In addition to being a friend, Rick has been my minister for more than a decade. I have learned much sitting at his feet and watching The Hills relentlessly pursue living out the mission of God as an American Bible-belt mega-church. The Hills demonstrates that many of the stereotypes of church models are inaccurate and unfair. It is what we are pursuing that matters most. There are many ways to be on mission as God's people.

I also need to thank several additional ministry friends who read an earlier version of this book and critiqued it for me. These include Jeff Hubbard, Brock Paulk, Curtis King, and Andy Johnson. They all offered me a rich engagement and good suggestions to improve the thinking and writing.

Our son Seth Bouchelle, who serves as a disciple maker and church planter in the Bronx, gave me some very helpful critique. I am inspired to see him living out so many of the principles I write about in this work. In a very real way, existing congregations can only adjust so much from their inherited identity and practices. We need to be involved in planting new models of church in collaboration with more traditional models and learn from each other. I learn much from Seth and the exciting work he is a part of in New York City.

Finally, I need to thank my wife Amy and other two children, Anna and Abby, who are constant conversation partners and endless encouragers. We actually talk about the subject of this book constantly in our family. They are all my teachers and can probably find some of their thoughts contained herein.

Thanks!

Dan Bouchelle
November 2021

Forward – By Dr. Leonard Allen

The truth is inescapable now: we are living in a time when a so-called "Christian America" has receded, even collapsed. Any sort of Christian cultural establishment has definitively passed away. And no one has been able to revive the corpse. Some believers take this development as a time for dark pessimism. But Christian faith, over its long history, has remained robust when it existed mostly outside the halls of power.

A surprisingly good thing about the cultural dislodging of Christian faith in the West is that it is forcing the church to rediscover its mission. And to rediscover the Holy Spirit of mission. A strong new sense of focus on and engagement in the mission is emerging. It is being forced upon us. We are having to decide if we are going to launch out on God's bold and demanding mission when Christian faith is not being sanctioned or propped up by our culture.

Let's say it plainly: in these times the church in the West is being shaken and dislodged from its ease and self-satisfaction. We are finding ourselves in a situation somewhat similar to Christians in the first three centuries. The early Christians occupied the margins of their culture and regularly found themselves odd outsiders, sometimes scorned, sometimes persecuted. But we face one big difference from them: they were introducing Christianity as a new and different religion; we face the challenge of reclaiming a faith "plagued by lukewarmness, division, worldliness, nationalism, and ignorance."[1]

The truth is that we now find ourselves in a missionary situation in our own culture. So, we are asking ourselves: Can we learn to think like missionaries in our own towns and cities? Can we see more clearly that mission is not one aspect of the church's life but the very centerpiece of what God is up to in the world? As Adrian Hastings put it, "The church of Christ does not so much have a mission as the mission of Christ has a church."

Dan Bouchelle's bold and timely book is just the kind of work we need to rethink the mission of God as we face the mounting challenges and pressures of a post-Christian Western culture. His study is deeply rooted in Scripture and structured around its master story. But

---

[1] Gerald Sittser, *Resilient Faith: How the Early Christian "Third Way" Changed the World* (Brazos, 2018), 18.

it is also richly informed by the perspective of the global church. He has observed closely the exploding Christian growth in the Global South or Majority World. He has mixed with streams of new believers, many from Muslim backgrounds, many from animistic backgrounds They are all caught up in the hope and joy of God's kingdom coming in Christ. One cannot miss how these disciples from "every tribe, nation, and tongue" transcend the boundaries of nation and politics. They wake one up and spin one's head around. One frequent traveler to the churches of the Global South captured the impact of the experience: after every trip I came back, he said, "humbled by my lack of faith, my own failure of imagination, and my resistance to committing myself to the high standard of being a servant of Christ."

From such perspective it's not hard to see North America as a mission field. Lesslie Newbigin over thirty years ago helped pioneer this focus, and a growing body of literature has emerged since the 1990s. Bouchelle well knows this work and draws upon it. He wants us to imagine moving beyond churches that send missionaries to being missional churches—churches caught up in the mission of God.

God's mission is to make all things new, to offer people reconciliation (both to God and to their enemies), and to (re)fashion creation as a place for human flourishing. The death and resurrection of Jesus is the crux, the pivot point. In this event, God's end-time age of righteousness and justice has erupted, unleashing "new creation." The Spirit of God is the sign, seal, and power of this emerging new creation. The Spirit enables us to participate in this cosmic missional project. Through the presence of the Holy Spirit, the church witnesses to the inbreaking of God's reign, tastes the banquet fare of the kingdom in advance, and becomes an instrument of God's kingdom by witnessing to and extending the ministry of Jesus.

In this strongly Bible-based study, Dan Bouchelle challenges, enlightens, and reframes the scope of how we think about God's mission. He broadens our understanding

- of the gospel to the full range of meanings found in Scripture,
- of salvation as a forgiving, mending, and renewing force for our world's multiplicitous brokenness,
- of mission as a holistic campaign for human forgiveness, deliverance, holiness, and flourishing,
- of how our political and nationalistic entanglements blunt and compromise the worldwide mission of the church,

- of how the Christian community is to be a contrast society to the political and cultural fray around us and to live as citizens of another commonwealth.

Christian communities are being shaken and forced to reconsider the mission. Can we learn to practice the faith without cultural privilege? Can we step out on God's mission in an increasingly secular—and often hostile—environment? These are bracing questions. This book provides a bracing guide.

Leonard Allen
Lipscomb University

Contents / Class Schedule

Preface:

We're on a Mission from God
By Dan Bouchelle

"A Church which has ceased to be a mission has lost
the essential character of a Church." - Lesslie Newbigin[2]

Most American Christians suffer from the "myth of saltwater[3]." That
is, we believe that "mission" is what happens across an ocean. Too
many American Christians also think of missions as something
reserved for special super-saints vastly unlike themselves. What we do
locally is merely "ministry." But, when pressed to clarify the difference
between mission and ministry, most people in the pew can't offer much
more than geography to distinguish them. In a globalized world, with
unprecedented immigration[4] and technology bringing all the world
together in new ways, and the nations from every continent having
moved in next door, the distinction between mission and ministry
makes less sense than ever.

This divide between missions and ministry was graphically displayed at
the university I attended for seminary. While I was working on my
MDiv, my alma mater built a brand-new "College of Biblical Studies"
building. It was big, beautiful, and state-of-the-art. It was large enough
to house all the related programs that had previously been scattered out
on campus. The most obvious separation had been between the
missions program and the ministry programs. They had been in
separate buildings before. Now they were combined, but not fully.

---

[2] Leonard Allen, *Poured Out*, page 173
[3] This helpful expression is borrowed from Paul Borthwick's *Western Christians in a Global Mission,* p. 57.
[4] Cf Jared Looney, *Crossroads of the Nations,* pp. 17-34, 47-56, Borthwick, pp. 32-79, and *Evangelical Missions Quarterly Vol. 56.4* "Globalization, Urbanization, Migration, and Rethinking the People Groups Concept," by Minh Ha Nguyen, pp. 32-35.

There was a big hallway in the new facility that separated the classrooms and offices of the two sides for missions and ministry.

While there was no discernable animosity between the programs, at least not that I noticed, the students and faculty were functionally different communities. We shared some classes, but everyone knew that the missions people and ministry people were on different paths that were almost different worlds. That mentality was not only unhelpful, but it was also harmful in ways that are still in play in much of the church.

For a select few American Christians, "mission" has become a special code word for getting outside the church's walls to serve those in the larger community. They talk about the church becoming "missional." But the "mission" they pursue often seems limited to humanitarian projects that look essentially identical to those of secular organizations or government, rather than something driven by a faith commitment. They can demonstrate the love of God, and we hope God gets some of the credit. But they do not have a clear intention or functioning strategy to turn the goodwill generated by their service of outsiders into life-transforming discipleship among those who are open to it.
Other American Christians tend to limit their understanding of "mission" to evangelistic efforts designed to make converts or plant churches. They are focused on passages like Matthew 28:16-20 and see the mission beginning with Jesus' final command and the establishment of what became "the church" as they have experienced it in American institutions. From this way of thinking, mission begins with a Bible study, climaxes in a baptistery, and ends in a set of rituals performed in an institution that follows some "pattern" of organization cobbled together from various New Testament passages. American Christians also typically only deal with people as individuals, and struggle to see or address larger issues of community transformation as the Kingdom of God emerges in the world.

All these perspectives contain genuine merit. Yet each fall well short of the full "mission of God," which is nothing less than the overarching story of God's work in our world that stretches from Genesis to Revelation and on to our day.

In this book, we will first seek to recapture a healthy understanding of what in the world God is doing and find ways to accept God's invitation to join his sweeping mission to redeem and restore all his creation. Secondly, we will seek to rediscover the "God of Mission" and the "Mission of God." Thirdly, we will be asking what God has been up to all these years, where he is going, and what our role is in this massive project. Finally, we will see that God's mission is as big as the universe and as long as eternity yet is so small it can be advanced on a short airplane ride or by giving a cup of cold water at just the right time.

Chapter 1:

From the Blues Brothers to Eternity
How We Got Lost While Seeking the Lost

What do you think of when you hear the word "mission?" Perhaps you picture an old Spanish mission like The Alamo, a mission statement from a business, a military campaign, or a cross-cultural religious worker on some distant continent. The language of mission is used so widely in our culture that it means both too much and too little. It lacks clear definition.

When we see someone focused and committed to some outcome we may say, "She is on a mission!" That typically means she is so driven to accomplish something that other matters just fade from her view. Does that language accurately reflect the way you see most Christians living out their faith?

I spent 22 years in congregational ministry with three churches in Texas and Oklahoma before accepting my current role with Mission Resource Network. For many of those years, I didn't really think about having a mission. I just assumed my job was to serve the church as I knew it and help it be more effective and more relevant in changing times. I thought my mission, to the degree I even used such language, was to help the church get better at doing what it was designed to do, not to question whether it had the right design at all.

Over time, I began to realize that the way I understood ministry was not working well and that I was missing something. My sense of mission was underdeveloped. I wasn't asking why the church exists in the first place. I wasn't asking what God was up to in the world or how the church was part of what he was doing beyond the church. I badly needed to rediscover the God of mission and mission of God so that I could serve well in a bigger story that would last longer than my life or the lives of the congregations I served for a while.

This takes me to one of my favorite movies from my youth: "The Blues Brothers." It is a farcical cult classic, but it is also memorable and quotable. I love the constant refrain of Jake and Elwood Blues,

"We are on a mission from God." Their mission drives the entire story. Behind all the wackiness, cameos by celebrities, and individual episodes throughout the movie is a singular mission to save the orphans' home that "saved" the Blues Brothers. In the early part of the movie, Jake and Elwood are "putting the band back together" to save the home. The characters that show up in this story are so colorful that the larger plot can be eclipsed at times. Yet, these characters are all part of an essential extended community of diverse personalities who come to the rescue of the orphans.

In a way, this is similar to the story of the Bible. At first blush, it can look like the Bible is nothing but a huge collection of small vignettes. It is easy to lose the larger narrative in the memorable characters and diverse scenes. But, through it all, there is a larger communal salvation story.

Do you think the American church can be accurately described as "on a mission from God?" While there are some congregations that have a strong sense of mission to impact the world beyond their members, this seems to be more an exception than the norm.

Actually, to say the church has a mission is not quite correct. It puts the church in the driver's seat and makes the church either the hero or the destination. The church does not save people. God does. The church is not just the freezer where we preserve the saved from spoiling until Jesus comes for them. It is more accurate to say that the church does not have a mission. God's mission has a church. Adrian Hastings put it this way, "The church of Christ does not so much have a mission as the mission of Christ has a church."[5] Put another way, Emil Brunner said, "The Church exists by mission, just as a fire exists by burning."[6]

God's mission predated the church. In fact, it predated all creation. Paul says as much in Ephesians 1:3-10, (NIV)

Praise be to the God and Father of our Lord Jesus Christ, who has blessed us in the heavenly realms with every spiritual blessing in Christ. For he chose us in him before the creation of the world to be holy and blameless in his sight. In love he predestined us for adoption to sonship through Jesus Christ, in accordance with his

---

[2]Leonard Allen, *Poured Out,* p. 97.
[6]Emil Brunner, *The Word in the World* (New York: Charles Scribner's Sons, 1931), p. 108.

pleasure and will—to the praise of his glorious grace, which he has freely given us in the One he loves. In him we have redemption through his blood, the forgiveness of sins, in accordance with the riches of God's grace that he lavished on us. With all wisdom and understanding, he made known to us the mystery of his will according to his good pleasure, which he purposed in Christ, to be put into effect when the times reach their fulfillment—to bring unity to all things in heaven and on earth under Christ.

Paul tells us God had a plan for our redemption before creating the world. The entire human story, and the whole of creation, has been part of God's purpose to display his glory in the heavenly realms. God has not been surprised or outplayed at any moment. He is fulfilling what he planned before he ever said, "Let there be light."

God had his mission in mind well before sin entered our world. While it is hard to know what all the planning of God before creation entails, and Christians have multiple explanations for what Paul means in Ephesians 1, it is clear that Jesus' coming into the world was not plan B which God was forced into by humanity's rebellion. Rather, Jesus' coming into our world was an essential part of God's plan. Human sin did not make God alter his purpose. Jesus was coming into the world from before the world was formed because God intended to show himself to us and do something among us that required his incarnation.

This means that God had planned for Jesus to suffer and die with and for us before he ever made us. God has been calling and using all his children to join him on that mission through all the many sub-narratives in the ultimate story that engulfs all of humanity and the world we inhabit.

While God's entire purpose was revealed in pieces over time and was still partly a mystery throughout the ages that preceded the coming of Jesus, God's global purpose was visible in part from early on. The mission of God really gets articulated for the first time in Genesis 12:1-3 (NIV)

The Lord had said to Abram, "Go from your country, your people and your father's household to the land I will show you. "I will make you into a great nation, and I will bless you; I will make your name great, and you will be a blessing. I will bless those who bless you, and whoever curses you I will curse; and all peoples on earth will be blessed through you."

The scope of Abram's call was always massive. It involved the blessing of all nations. That seemed stunning at that time in history. How could one man be a blessing to all nations? How would this be possible, especially before modern transportation and communication technologies when everything was so local? Keep reading. The rest of the Bible answers these questions even if it seems to focus mostly on a single small nation in a narrow, vulnerable corridor in the ancient world. The Bible is the story of God's mission from before creation until the fulfillment to come at Jesus' second appearing.

The Gospel starts early in Genesis and runs through the Old Testament. It is an epic tale of how God created a world and a people made in his image to rule over creation for him. It explains how we rejected God's rightful reign in Eden, tried to make the world submit to us instead of to God, and turned creation from a source of boundless life and joy in a cursed place of unending conflict and death. It is the story of the call of Abraham and development of his family into God's instrument to reintroduce himself to his world. It reveals God's character through his long relationship with the nation of Israel. It demonstrates how trustworthy and long-suffering is this loving and holy God, who has been pursuing us, and his dream to redeem and restore his world. This was God's plan from before creation and he has never deviated from it.

The scope of the story starts coming into clearer focus when we get to the New Testament. The Gospels all make the bold claim that Jesus is the next step in the story of God found in the OT. Luke and Acts in particular make this clear. Jesus is the continuation of the story of Israel and the church is the ongoing story of Jesus in the world.

This is especially clear from the first two verses of Acts 1:1-2 (NIV):

In my former book, Theophilus, I wrote about all that Jesus began to do and to teach until the day he was taken up to heaven, after giving instructions through the Holy Spirit to the apostles he had chosen.

Notice that Luke refers to all Jesus "began" to do and teach. Jesus isn't done. He continues his work and teaching through his people who contain his Spirit. Notice also that at the end of this book in Acts 28, Luke does not bring the story to a conclusion, but merely leaves Paul awaiting trial. Why is this? Because the story has not been completed. We are still writing chapters. We live in Acts 29. God's mission continues through us.

Unfortunately, the church in the United States and most of the western world lost its sense of mission. Christianity in an institutional sense got so enmeshed into the culture of Europe and former European colonies that we forgot what story we were in. Mission became what happened in pagan countries. We thought we lived in a Christian country where almost everyone believed in God and our role was to make sure people got their doctrine and rituals right. The church became focused on making sure individuals went to heaven and enjoyed the afterlife because the work of announcing the good news was done. Now we are just trying to ensure the saved stay saved or live like the saved.[7]

It seemed as if the mission was largely complete in our part of the world. Anyone who was still lost must just want to be lost. The church was here if they wanted God. The church became the nanny of the state or culture, which wagged a finger in the face of people saying, "You should not be doing that." In a "Christian culture" we thought of ourselves as the "moral majority." This is our country and our culture. I fear, in large part, we've lost our sense of mission as people of another kingdom and traded it for a sense of entitlement as citizens of a "Christian culture."

But the reality is that Americans do not live in a Christian culture, and the church is living in denial if we think our objective is just to increase market share and be moral nannies. We must get over the myth of saltwater. Mission isn't just something that happens across an ocean. It is what we are called to live out everywhere all the time. There is no transformation by aviation. Putting people on an airplane won't turn them into missionaries any more than kittens climbing into an oven will

---

[7] If this line of thought is new and challenging to you, I'd suggest you read *Forgotten Ways*, by Alan Hirsch, *The King Jesus Gospel*, by Scott McKnight, and *Canoeing the Mountains*, by Tod Bolsinger.

turn them into biscuits. People in churches need help to remember what story we are in and how to live out our roles in this story at this time.

God's mission is not about getting lost people in the church; it is about getting Christ in lost people. It is about joining the Christ in drawing all people into the fullness of his person and mission. God's mission is to establish his reign everywhere, transforming people at every level of every society in every aspect of life in both the heavens and earth so that all things live out the full beauty of God's character of love and shalom.

Instead of grieving the church's loss of institutional status in America, the "post-Christian" status of our culture could end up being the salvation of the church if we respond properly. The purpose of the church is not to make any nation better.[8] Rather, it is to invite people to join God's kingdom people, a holy nation unlike any of this world, so that we may live as citizens of a better kingdom. We need to wake up to our purpose and move beyond institutional visions to kingdom visions. It is time for us to rediscover the mission of God so that the church can get put back in its proper place as the instrument of God's mission in the world. It is time we refocus the church by rediscovering

---

[8] It is hard for us to talk about nations today without getting confused. Nations in scripture are not the same thing as nations in the modern sense of "nation-state." The way we think of nations today is a product of the modern era. Historically speaking, "nations" were people groups with a common culture, history (story), and language. They had a sense of us v. them. They typically, but not always, had territory they occupied, but their borders were often ill-defined, disputed, and flexible. Nations were not products of law, like today. There were no constitutions in the days of scripture. Nations often had kings and were partly defined by who reigned over them. But, many "nations" were just people groups with tribal chiefs or clan leaders and no king as we think of them or defined lands. It is probably better for us today to think of nations in terms of the Cherokee Nation or Comanche Nation in US history. Even among ancient nations with kings, there typically resided people groups (other "nations") mixed in within them who were not part of the dominant culture, like Ruth, a Moabitess among Israel. When I speak of nations throughout this book, I'm speaking of people groups or ethnicities, and not legal nation-states. When I speak of God's nation, I am not ever speaking of the USA or any legally constructed nation state. Rather, I'm speaking of God's multi-ethnic people who dwell in many countries. God's nation is all those who recognize and submit to his reign. This is similar but not identical with the way we use the word church. But the word church has many meanings in English which contribute to confusion as well.

10

our mission. All believers are called to continue the mission of God until all things are redeemed and brought under the Lordship of Jesus.

Putting this into practice
1. Begin to take note of how often you hear Christians talking in ways that confuse Kingdom of God with the United States of America or whatever your home country is. Keep a running list in a journal over a period of weeks and reflect on the implications of the failure to distinguish between the two.
2. Make a list of the people you know in your world who are far from God and begin praying for God to create an opportunity for you to have a spiritual conversation with them.
3. Begin making a list of people you encounter who come from very different communities—who seem socially remote to you—and who are unlikely to be Christians. Just start gathering information and raising your awareness of how many people you encounter every week who are "not your people."

Chapter 2:

Where Is the Map?
A Travel Guide for People on Mission

I come from a fellowship of churches that prides itself on Bible knowledge and faithfulness to the "pattern of scripture." Preachers were measured by how much Bible we cited. Everything we did needed biblical precedent or at least a clear biblical mandate. Any idea or program proposed first had to prove its biblical bona fides if it expected to gain any traction with our people. We were deeply committed to being biblical, but we did not agree on what made something biblical. So, we spent a lot of time wrestling over how to interpret the library of books that made up our Bibles, because the goal of being biblical is hardly a precise target.

There are few words as confusing as "biblical." Christians of many tribes talk as if everyone knows what being "biblical" means when it really has many meanings that get all mixed up together. We talk about "biblical values" or "biblical ideas" as if that is one clear set of things. We talk like doing things in the biblical way is so obvious and clear that we don't have to explain or define it, but that isn't true.

For example, one biblical model for marriage is for a widow to marry her dead husband's brother and raise children who are counted as the late husband's children (Gen. 38:6-10). It is also biblical for women who are prisoners of war to be taken as additional wives or concubines of conquering warriors (Num. 31:1-18 & Deut. 21:11-14). Oh, then there is the biblical practice of concubines in the first place. It is a good biblical move for a man to marry his half-sister but have her tell people she is his sister instead of his wife when he is traveling abroad (Gen. 12:10-20). These examples may seem extreme and even humorous today, but they are straightforward biblical models. Yet, you don't typically hear people citing them today as examples to follow. At least, let's hope not.

In reality, the Bible is a complex collection of 66 books written over more than 1000 years addressing many different situations. Using the Bible correctly requires some instruction and healthy models.

13

When we don't know how to use scripture, the mission of God gets lost or distorted. To recover our mission, the church must first recover our understanding of scripture as the story of God's mission to redeem and restore his world.

In churches with a high view of inspiration, we can easily get confused about the purpose of the Bible and turn the church into a school where just teaching the Bible is the primary purpose. We think the goal is to get scripture into people's minds instead of getting Jesus' character in their lives.

Too many Christians have an "Islamic" understanding of the Bible. I know that sounds bizarre. But, let me explain what I mean. For Muslims, the Quran provides the words of Allah as dictated to Mohammed. Mohammed is very important and highly honored, but ultimately, he is just a human being. He was a prophet God used to bring us the real gift of revelation in the form of a holy book. The Quran is miraculously perfect and is venerated as our path to God. It is an oversimplification, but you could say that Islam is a man pointing at a book.

For Christians, Jesus himself is the supreme Word of God. Our scriptures, the Old and New Testaments, are merely instruments to help us understand God. The focus is not on the Bible itself, but on the God revealed through the Bible. Our Bible provides us a diverse set of windows we look through to see God and his purpose from many angles over time. We don't look at windows. We look through windows. In contrast to Islam, in Christianity we have a book pointing at a man.[9] We don't worship the Bible. Christians worship the God revealed in the Bible. Jesus said as much in John 5:39-40 (NIV):

> You study the Scriptures diligently because you think that in them you have eternal life. These are the very Scriptures that testify about me, yet you refuse to come to me to have life.

There are many misconceptions about the Bible that distract us from finding our purpose. To followers of Jesus, the Bible is often seen as one or more of the following:

---

[9] This contrast is not original to me, but I no longer know where I picked it up.

1. A list of rules and rituals, or a legal constitution, telling us how to do church right (especially worship) that we must obey correctly to go to heaven when we die.
2. A set of morality stories designed to show us how to be good.
3. An encyclopedia or textbook for philosophy, science, or history designed to answer any question we bring to it—the ultimate answer book.
4. A talisman or magical/holy book that we carry and honor as a symbol of God's presence with us.

If you have been a Christian very long, you have probably seen each of these distorted views of scripture play out in real life. The results for the church and its mission range from annoying to disastrous when we use scripture in these ways.

The scriptures themselves tell us how to use the Bible. In Hebrews 1:1-3 the writer contrasts the way God spoke to people through the centuries before Jesus with how he has revealed himself more completely in the person of his incarnate son.

> In the past God spoke to our ancestors through the prophets at many times and in various ways, but in these last days he has spoken to us by his Son, whom he appointed heir of all things, and through whom also he made the universe. The Son is the radiance of God's glory and the exact representation of his being, sustaining all things by his powerful word. After he had provided purification for sins, he sat down at the right hand of the Majesty in heaven. (NIV)

Something more significant than written revelation has happened with the coming of Jesus. His appearance in the world changes how we know and relate to God and his will ever since.

John says something similar in his prologue John 1:1-14 (NIV);

> In the beginning was the Word, and the Word was with God, and the Word was God. He was with God in the beginning. Through him all things were made; without him nothing was made that has been made. In him was life, and that life was the light of all mankind. The light shines in the darkness, and the darkness has not overcome it.

15

There was a man sent from God whose name was John. He came as a witness to testify concerning that light, so that through him all might believe. He himself was not the light; he came only as a witness to the light.

The true light that gives light to everyone was coming into the world. He was in the world, and though the world was made through him, the world did not recognize him. He came to that which was his own, but his own did not receive him. Yet to all who did receive him, to those who believed in his name, he gave the right to become children of God— children born not of natural descent, nor of human decision or a husband's will, but born of God.

The Word became flesh and made his dwelling among us. We have seen his glory, the glory of the one and only Son, who came from the Father, full of grace and truth.

If we want to know God and relate to him in the most intimate and accurate way, we don't need to look at a book but at a person—the fullness of God who came in Jesus. The point for us after the coming of Jesus is not to know all the words and keep all of the rules, but to continue the life-model of the one who shows us who God is and how he behaves. We follow a person, not a book.

In our love of the Bible, we can get lost in scripture study and miss the point. This could not be clearer in what Jesus said himself in John 5:39-40 (NIV),

You study the Scriptures diligently because you think that in them you have eternal life. These are the very Scriptures that testify about me, yet you refuse to come to me to have life.

Jesus condemned biblical scholars of his day who loved to study scripture and thought life was found in a book but missed the entire point—God has shown us who he is and how he wants us to live in Jesus.

The will of God, and the mission of God, is rooted primarily in God's character and only secondarily in scripture. We understand our mission by reflecting on the nature of our God, which involves more than a scripture study. It is a living relationship with a person that involves not only the written word, but also an indwelling spiritual connection to the person of God's Son. We can only understand how to live into the Christ-story by a healthy practice of reading about and reflecting on God's character as revealed in the scriptures over the centuries, lived out in communities of faith, as guided by God's Spirit. Our model is not a book but a person. Jesus shows us what God is like and what humanity can and should be.

The Bible is not primarily a rule book to obey or a collection of advice to implement, but it is a story to live. Scripture is the story of God's pursuit of his mission through many generations of Abraham's family to reach all families of the world. Not everything that happens, and not everything God does in these stories, is normative today. We don't serve God's story well by copying everything we see in the story, but by continuing to pursue what God has been pursuing from the beginning. We are not seeking to relive earlier moments in the story. We are seeking to live out God's character and purpose in our lives as the story progresses to the end God has been leading humanity toward from the beginning. Our faith is not backwards facing but forward leaning. We are called to live into the conclusion of the story in the present. We are not trying to recapture Eden or replicate all the mundane practices of some golden era of the church (as if there was some period when the church got everything right).[10] We are rather seeking to be the best approximation of Jesus and his future people today. I'll have far more to say about this later in this book. But for now, let me say that how we read the whole Bible is shaped by how we expect the story to end. Those who believe the end is an escape will read the Bible differently from those who believe the end is a restoration.

The entire Bible (OT & NT) finds its focus and fulfillment in Jesus' life, death, resurrection, and commission to make disciples of all nations. **Jesus is the lens through which we read all scripture.** Everything before Jesus leads up to him and everything after flows from him.

This is essential for our understanding and practice when dealing with many difficult passages in the OT, such as calls for genocide,

---

[10] For more on this idea, please see *Illusions of Innocence*, by Leonard Allen and Richard Hughes. This book was life transforming for me.

commands to engage in holy war, and many practices associated with ancient cultural and worship practices. In all matters, we need to start with Jesus' life and teachings (e.g., the Sermon on the Mount) which is our core understanding of the life God calls us to live. Only as we understand Jesus can we properly deal with the things that came before. God has revealed himself in a gradual or progressive way.

Many elements found in the story, from an earlier stage in God's work, were accommodations to the limits of the people God was working with and are no longer appropriate for us. Just like parents unintentionally distort things in explaining them to children who can't yet grasp their complexity, which they later have to clarify, God brought humanity along at the pace we could understand him. What he revealed to us was true, but not clear until the rest of the story unfolded. When parents tell a two-year-old not to touch the stove, they don't mean to prohibit cooking when that child grows up. But, a two-year-old can't understand when it is appropriate to touch a stove and when it's not. So, at that stage of development, you just say, "Don't touch." That is not a good word for the mature.

Just so, God's earliest revelations of himself have to take into consideration the developmental level of his people and not get stuck in immature stages of understanding before the full revelation we get in Jesus. Having a developmental understanding of God's revelation keeps us from misusing scripture in ways that are "out of date" or part of a time period that has been surpassed because of God's later and greater revelation in Jesus.[11]

We need to be careful here. The Old Testament is more than historical background to the NT; it is part of the grand narrative of God's work to redeem and restore all nations. While many elements in it are surpassed by later revelation, the overarching narrative is essential for understanding God and his faithful character and purpose over time.

The story of Jesus encountering some of his confused disciples after his resurrection on the road to Emmaus in Luke 24:13-27, 44-49 is

---

[11] This is particularly important with events like the conquest of Canaan, holy wars, and rules about putting the ban on conquered peoples, which involved their total annihilation. These are difficult issues which require complex answers beyond the scope of this book. However, a couple of helpful resources are Lee Camp's *Scandalous Witness* and Gregory A. Boyd's *God at War*.

helpful. Jesus helped them rethink the entirety of the OT scriptures in light of his life, death, and resurrection. The themes of God's suffering with and for his people, the sacrifices and symbolism of the temple which pointed to Jesus, God's passion for the unity of all nations, the anticipation for what Jesus would do was woven through the Old Testament, but they had just not seen it. But once Jesus opened their eyes to what was in their own scriptures, they couldn't not see it. How could they have missed it? Finally, the pieces came together, and God's purpose was clear. As Paul says often, much of what God was doing in the world was a mystery until Jesus came. Afterwards, the mystery was revealed (e.g., 1 Cor. 2:7, Eph. 1:9, 3:3-9, and Col. 1:26-27).

The OT scriptures were true and helpful in many ways, but they were not adequate to reveal what God was doing in the world without seeing Jesus' death, burial, and resurrection. Only after Jesus' passion does the overarching purpose of God in history come into focus.

When we come to understand what God is doing through the lens of Jesus, everything comes into focus and our purpose becomes clearer— to draw people to Jesus and draw them into his life and mission. For the Christian, we don't start with the OT and work our way to Jesus. We start with Jesus and then read the OT through his life and teaching.[12] It is a cyclical, not a linear, process. When we do this, we see that God is powerful and while his power can be useful in war at times, God is not fundamentally a God of war, but a God of love. We see that God may have helped Israel deal with enemy nations that posed a threat to them, but his ultimate goal was not the destruction of the other nations, but the restoration and unification of all nations. It is one thing for you to pray for God to help you defend yourself against someone who breaks into your home to do you harm, but that does not mean you should expect God to empower you to defeat anyone you choose to fight.

We are people who live out Jesus' story and make him visible in the world so people can find their life and purpose in him. As much as we love scripture, the only scripture many people see is through our lives,

---

[12] I realize that this involves breaking with one of the orthodoxies of historical-critical scholarship. In saying this, I'm not saying there is no legitimate place for the study and interpretation of OT texts in their contexts. However, for Christians to hear them as God's Word to us today, we have to read them through the lens of God's more complete revelation in Christ in whom all wisdom is found.

and that's okay for a start. The goal isn't to get the Bible in people, but to introduce them to Christ and get Christ in them. That starts with you, not a Bible study in most cases.

Before we invite anyone into a Bible study, we have to form enough relationship to earn their trust by being with them in a gracious way. That will probably cause us to get criticized just like Jesus was because we are often with the wrong people and appear to be condoning things God has rejected. When we do begin to talk, we need to start with having normal conversations about regular stuff where we listen well and demonstrate authentic interest in others and the things going on in their life. Our son Seth leads a team of disciple-makers and church planters working with the diverse people groups in New York City. In his evangelism training he says, "You can't have a spiritual conversation if you can't have a conversation."

Only when we get to know people and what concerns them will we know where to start getting them connected to scripture. Scripture is important, but it doesn't replace people and relationships. It points us to a relationship with Jesus, who is God's word for us.

Putting this into practice

Try to have a meaningful conversation with someone outside your normal friend or co-worker group this week. Don't try to move it toward a spiritual direction unless that happens naturally. Just start connecting and showing interest in the lives of people you don't normally talk to who don't know Jesus. Then, when you begin to talk beyond surface matters and into deeper life issues, you can naturally share what matters to you and God will come up naturally. If you don't push but draw people in over time, there is no telling where that can lead.

If you are able to get someone interested in reading scripture with you, avoid being the teacher with all the answers. Stay in the guide role instead of expert role by suggesting scriptures and asking questions and then letting them find answers in the scripture. Here are some good questions to use in any Bible study when you find someone interested in reading scripture with you. Questions such as these allow the Word to be the teacher and avoid making you the expert.

1. What does this passage tell us about God?
2. What does this passage tell us about Jesus (if he is in the story)?
3. What in this passage is good news for you and your people?
4. How can we best obey this in order to be like Jesus?
5. Who can we share this with?

Chapter 3:

The Only True Bible Hero
The God of Mission

One of the big surprises to me about our culture right now is the popularity of comic book-based Superhero movies. Superman, Batman, and maybe Spiderman didn't surprise me. But all the other characters who have been featured in major motion pictures, many of whom I've barely heard of, do surprise me. We've seen blockbusters with sequels for characters like Iron Man, Wonder Woman, Thor, X-men, Black Panther, and on and on. Why is this so prevalent? Why now? What does this need for an unrealistic hero set in a simplistic story tell us about ourselves and our contemporary culture? Isn't this a rather childish trend?

It's not that I don't recognize the appeal of a hero or superhero. We've all felt that tug. When I was growing up, I was obsessed with the Lone Ranger. My granddad was a farmer and rancher. Combining the western gunfighter with a superhero was particularly appealing to me. But, at some point, I gave up looking for two-dimensional heroes to arise in our world. I got jaded and Clint Eastwood's anti-hero characters seemed more realistic. I came to believe that humans were too deeply flawed to save themselves, even if we did acquire special powers from the bite of a radioactive spider, like Peter Parker, or develop cool weapons with massive amounts of money and technology like Bruce Wayne or Tony Stark.

While I gave up on secular superheroes, I still longed for heroes and it was tempting to look for them in the Bible. I grew up on Bible heroes who got their special power from God. That's what I thought we needed: another Moses, David, Daniel, or Paul. I was told in church that I could be that next hero if I was a good boy. That didn't seem believable because I had met myself. But God might raise up another hero like the Bible characters of old if we were all very pious.

Yet, the more I read the Bible, the more I saw the same pattern with Bible characters as I did with secular superheroes. They were not realistic. It's not that they didn't exist, like the comic book types, but that they turned out not to be so heroic after all.

All the Bible heroes were seriously flawed people when I looked closely. Adam and Eve broke God's law, turned on each other, and then got deported. Cain killed Abel. Noah got drunk and acted shamefully, then disgraced and cursed his son when he got caught. Abraham lied about his wife, put the promise of God in jeopardy, and tried to bypass God's plan with Hagar and Ishmael. Isaac and Rebecca showed favoritism and fought over which son should be the heir of God's promises. Jacob lied, cheated, and stole most of his life. All the patriarchs were polygamists. Reuben raped his stepmother. Simeon and Levi deceived and massacred a village. Judah had incest with his daughter-in-law. Ten of Jacob's sons sold Joseph into slavery and lied to Jacob about it. Moses was a murderer, lost his temper in a self-righteous tirade, and arrogantly claimed credit for God's work. Aaron made the golden calf that Israel worshipped while Moses was receiving the law of God. Gideon was a coward and was complicit in the later developing of idolatry. Samson visited prostitutes and violated his oath. Saul betrayed God and tried to kill David. David was an adulterer, murderer, and violent ruler who indulged his children and brought the kingdom to civil war. Solomon became arrogant and self-indulgent and openly brought idolatry to Israel in order to pacify his hundreds of foreign wives God had forbidden in the first place. Need I go on?

Ironically, the most honorable characters in scripture seemed to be women like Deborah, Hanna, Huldah, Mary and the other women who followed Jesus and didn't abandon him at the cross. But even among the women, there were problems. For example, Miriam was overcome with jealousy of Moses' position and was stricken with leprosy. Despite their superior performance in scripture, none of the female characters were towering figures of strength that could be held up as a superhero either. Even Mary thought Jesus was out of his mind and tried to derail his ministry on one occasion.

It seemed like the people God used to advance his mission through the ages turned out to be tragically weak or flawed, just like me, when viewed closely. The more deeply we read scripture, the clearer it becomes that while God has used many people through the ages to advance his mission, they were all profoundly limited. God alone is the only true hero of every story.

24

Just look at the following scriptures to get a sampling of this theme: Isaiah 40:12-31(NIV)

Who has measured the waters in the hollow of his hand,
    or with the breadth of his hand marked off the heavens?
Who has held the dust of the earth in a basket,
    or weighed the mountains on the scales
    and the hills in a balance?
Who can fathom the Spirit of the Lord,
    or instruct the Lord as his counselor?
Whom did the Lord consult to enlighten him,
    and who taught him the right way?
Who was it that taught him knowledge,
    or showed him the path of understanding?
Surely the nations are like a drop in a bucket;
    they are regarded as dust on the scales;
    he weighs the islands as though they were fine dust.
Lebanon is not sufficient for altar fires,
    nor its animals enough for burnt offerings.
Before him all the nations are as nothing;
    they are regarded by him as worthless
    and less than nothing.
With whom, then, will you compare God?
    To what image will you liken him?
As for an idol, a metalworker casts it,
    and a goldsmith overlays it with gold
    and fashions silver chains for it.
A person too poor to present such an offering
    selects wood that will not rot;
they look for a skilled worker
    to set up an idol that will not topple.
Do you not know?
    Have you not heard?
Has it not been told you from the beginning?
    Have you not understood since the earth was founded?
He sits enthroned above the circle of the earth,
    and its people are like grasshoppers.
He stretches out the heavens like a canopy,

and spreads them out like a tent to live in.
He brings princes to naught
  and reduces the rulers of this world to nothing.
No sooner are they planted,
  no sooner are they sown,
  no sooner do they take root in the ground,
than he blows on them and they wither,
  and a whirlwind sweeps them away like chaff.
"To whom will you compare me?
  Or who is my equal?" says the Holy One.
Lift up your eyes and look to the heavens:
  Who created all these?
He who brings out the starry host one by one
  and calls forth each of them by name.
Because of his great power and mighty strength,
  not one of them is missing.
Why do you complain, Jacob?
  Why do you say, Israel,
"My way is hidden from the Lord;
  my cause is disregarded by my God"?
Do you not know?
  Have you not heard?
The Lord is the everlasting God,
  the Creator of the ends of the earth.
He will not grow tired or weary,
  and his understanding no one can fathom.
He gives strength to the weary
  and increases the power of the weak.
Even youths grow tired and weary,
  and young men stumble and fall;
but those who hope in the Lord
  will renew their strength.
They will soar on wings like eagles;
  they will run and not grow weary,
  they will walk and not be faint.

Isaiah graphically reminds us that the Lord is incomparable. He is more powerful and more enduring even than the great empires of the world. They are like the water drops that fall from a bucket unnoticed and not missed. He alone rules from on high and there is no other power or source of hope besides him. God acts as he wills for his own sake and for his own honor. He does not share his glory with any rivals. This is a common theme in the Psalms and the prophets and is woven throughout the Old Testament.

When Jesus comes, he sings a second verse to this same song, with a focus on God's work through him. Even as Jesus is preparing his apostles, he makes it clear who the hero is in Luke 10:1-12. (NIV)

> After this the Lord appointed seventy-two others and sent them two by two ahead of him to every town and place where he was about to go. He told them, "The harvest is plentiful, but the workers are few. Ask the Lord of the harvest, therefore, to send out workers into his harvest field. Go! I am sending you out like lambs among wolves. Do not take a purse or bag or sandals; and do not greet anyone on the road. "When you enter a house, first say, 'Peace to this house.' If someone who promotes peace is there, your peace will rest on them; if not, it will return to you. Stay there, eating and drinking whatever they give you, for the worker deserves his wages. Do not move around from house to house.
> "When you enter a town and are welcomed, eat what is offered to you. Heal the sick who are there and tell them, 'The kingdom of God has come near to you.' But when you enter a town and are not welcomed, go into its streets and say, 'Even the dust of your town we wipe from our feet as a warning to you. Yet be sure of this: The kingdom of God has come near.' I tell you, it will be more bearable on that day for Sodom than for that town.

Jesus' followers can be workers and witnesses, but only the Lord of the Harvest can produce fruit. Humans can bear witness to the coming Kingdom, but only the King can save us and our world. We can pray, go out in the name of the Lord, and look for the people God has already been preparing, i.e., people of peace.[13] But the Lord must show up to bring in the long-awaited Kingdom.

Paul is equally clear about who the hero is, and it isn't him. In Philippians 2:5-11 (NIV)

In your relationships with one another, have the same mindset as Christ Jesus:
　Who, being in very nature God,
　did not consider equality with God something to be used to his own advantage;
rather, he made himself nothing
　by taking the very nature of a servant,
　being made in human likeness.
And being found in appearance as a man,
　he humbled himself
　by becoming obedient to death—
　　even death on a cross!
　Therefore God exalted him to the highest place
　and gave him the name that is above every name,
that at the name of Jesus every knee should bow,
　in heaven and on earth and under the earth,
and every tongue acknowledge that Jesus Christ is Lord,
　to the glory of God the Father.

Paul makes it clear that God, acting through Jesus' life, death, burial, and resurrection, is restoring the world. When it is all done, all glory will be to the one hero. Paul tells us in places like Ephesians 2:10 that we have a role, but it is only as God's workmanship, not the craftsman himself. God forms us into useful partners in his work. But we are formed in Christ to do the work he has long planned and prepared for us to do. Only to the degree that we are extensions of Jesus through his Spirit working in us and through us as he directs us can humans be part of this salvation story.

Such an invitation both dignifies and humbles us. We can be useful to God's mission because he works in us. But only because he is at

---

[13] See Luke 10:1-12

work in us, and to the degree that we are in step with his Spirit and working in his power, can we be useful.

This is illustrated well in the story from John 4 at the well outside the Samaritan village of Sychar as Jesus draws into service a woman without a resume (or one of the wrong kind) who would have been overlooked by everyone in her day. Jesus uses her to draw the attention of an entire village that would have been completely written off by Jesus' Jewish disciples. In the wrap up of the story, Jesus tells his disciples to look around and recognize that even in religiously compromised Samaria, the fields were ready for harvest.

How is that possible? Jesus and the disciples just arrived. Who has cleared the field, planted a crop, and nurtured it to the point of harvest? God did. He is already working everywhere in ways we cannot see.

Because this is God's world and he has never abandoned it, we always step into an existing God story no matter where we go and how godforsaken it looks to us. There are signs of God's presence everywhere. He is always preparing people to hunger for him and hear from him before he sends any of us there to be human witnesses.

In Genesis 14 and Exodus 18, Abraham encounters Melchizedek, and Moses meets with Jethro. Both are priests who are honored as sources of wisdom, but they are not part of God's primary storyline. They are not in the family of Abraham or in God's covenant people. How can these people know anything about God? Because God is working in ways we don't recognize, and evidence of his presence can be found everywhere.

No one gets everything wrong. That doesn't mean they don't need more of the story, but it does mean that the first servant of God to show up isn't the hero. He or she is merely the witness to the hero who has been there before they showed up and has been preparing the way and reaching out in ways the people there don't yet understand.

Being able to distinguish God's role and our role is essential if we want to be effective in our role. It keeps us from being arrogant and presumptuous. It also gives us confidence to go places that we would never take on in our own power and do things that seem impossible without God's presence and empowerment.

Our role in God's work is like John the Baptist in John 1. We point to the light, prepare the way for God, testify to the one who comes after us, and then get out of his way. We are not called to be the judge or lawyers but merely witnesses (Acts 1:7-8). But we need to do our job well and trust the judge to establish justice. The question for us is: How can we put in a good word for God with others without condemning them, shaming them, or communicating judgement?

If we understand that God is on mission everywhere before we go anywhere—and he is working on us to prepare us for the work, and is preparing the people and moments before we arrive, and that he works in us—why would we be intimidated to join his work? What holds us back from making the turn in conversations to a spiritual direction?

That is exactly what Paul tells us God does in Ephesians 2:10 (NIV):

> For we are God's handiwork, created in Christ Jesus to do good works, which God prepared in advance for us to do.

Remember, everywhere we go, God has already been, and he is never without some level of witness, even though it may be muted or distorted. God goes before us to prepare the way. Our job is to discover what God is doing and how we join it. We are not the source of the light, we merely point to the Light. We do not save, we merely announce the coming of the Savior. **Instead of asking "What would Jesus do?" we might be better off asking "What would John the Baptist do?" because we prepare the way for the Lord instead of seeking to be him in the lives of others.**

In our ministry at Mission Resource Network, we have seen this over and over with missionaries around the world. In recent years, we have heard more stories than we can count about Muslim background believers in Jesus who took their first steps toward Jesus after he appeared to them in a dream or vision. To a woman who was a baker, he said "I am the bread of life." To a refugee who fell asleep on the sidewalk while waiting for a food ministry to open, he said, "I am the door and the door is open."

To a young man in North Africa he appeared in three dreams in the same night. First, he showed up surrounded by angels singing hallelujah (a word he did not know before) and told him he loved him. In the second dream he appeared with the marks of the cross on his body and told him "drink my blood and eat my body." In the third,

30

Jesus told him, "You will be my spokesman." This man sought out a Christian online, read the book of Matthew overnight, and was baptized the next day. He then lost his job, was beaten up by his family, and stabbed in an attack by the Muslim Brotherhood. Yet, he boldly testified in court about his faith in Jesus in the subsequent trial where his attackers were convicted. He was later commended by the judge privately after the trial.

While these seem like unusual cases, and in some sense they are, though not as odd as you probably think, they illustrate that God is working everywhere. He doesn't do the same thing everywhere all the time, but he is active. They show why prayer and spiritual discernment are not preparations for our mission, they are mission work.

Since God is the Lord of the Harvest, and we are mere field hands who serve him, we need to be careful not to put some people on pedestals. That puts too much pressure on them and takes too much responsibility off the rest of us.

Before we try to enlighten others, whom we presume need our unique wisdom, we should be looking for signs of God's work in them before we ever arrived. Instead of going all over the world looking only for what is missing that we can bring, we should start by looking for what good is already present that we can learn from, affirm, and work with to advance God's mission. Instead of assuming we can save others, we should look for ways to serve them and earn their trust so that we can point them toward the one who is saving all of us. Instead of assuming that mission flows from the West to the rest (as if Western culture is godly and all other cultures are broken), we need to recognize that God is Lord of all the earth and that all cultures are mixtures of his common grace and brokenness in need of God's saving grace.

This does not diminish our mission; it sets it in proper perspective. The gospel is not our mission, it is God's mission. We are merely servants as we follow God on mission with people and in places he has been preparing long before we arrive.

Putting this into practice

1. Go back over the lists you've been making. How are you doing with forming relationships and having conversations with those people?
2. Think about how you can put in a good word for God with others without confronting them, shaming them, or communicating judgement. What are some natural conversational moves you can make to turn conversations toward spiritual matters without it being forced?
3. If we understand that God is on mission everywhere before we go anywhere—and he is working on us to prepare us for the work, and is preparing the people and moments before we arrive, and that he works in us—why would we be intimidated to join his work? Reflect on what holds you back from making the turn in conversations to a spiritual direction? Make a list and ask yourself how legitimate those fears are.
4. Pray this week for God to create opportunities for you to talk to someone who is seeking him and for God to reveal persons of peace to you.

Chapter 4:

Mission #1: Restoration of God's Image
Why You Should Stop Trying to Go to Heaven

We have a common saying in American culture that goes like this, "I'm only human." Often it is used this way: "What do you expect? I'm only human." Think about this a minute. What does this saying mean? When do we tend to say this? It usually follows a confrontation where we've been forced to face our fallibility. We are claiming that we should not be held up to an impossible standard because we are not divine. We are only weak and mistake-prone creatures.

This saying implies that everyone should know that humans are error prone and, therefore, we should not expect too much of each other. It assumes something like a belief in the fall of humanity or original sin. It recognizes there is a standard from somewhere that we can't meet even if we feel obligated to do so. It reveals that we feel shame about our weakness even though we don't think it is fair for us to be held to a flawless standard. That is a complex set of ideas and feelings rolled up into a common phrase we use without even thinking much about it.

Now think about what it means for us to use the language of salvation. What does it mean to "be saved" or "get saved." What does "being saved" involve? Saved from what? When are we saved? How does it change us? Does it change who we are now, or does it only change our eternal destination?

While it may seem like asking what it means to be human and what it means to be saved are unrelated, they really aren't if we understand the scriptures and especially the gospel. Humans are composite creatures. We are neither angels nor animals. Unlike angels, we have material bodies made from dirt. The name "Adam" literally means dirt. It refers to the material from which humans are formed in the Genesis 2 story. To call the first man Adam would be like calling him "Clod," "Dirtling," or "Dusty."

In the creation narrative, humans are both like and unlike the animals. Like the other creatures, we are created by God on the 6th day to live on the dirt (dry ground) and we share many characteristics. We inhabit bodies. We eat, sleep, procreate, and die. We depend on our environment for nourishment and are threatened by nature and other creatures.

However, unlike the animals, we don't just live off what the land and natural surroundings produce. We are constantly trying to change the world around us to draw more from it than it wants to surrender. We "work" for a living instead of just striving to exist. In the process, we imagine with great longing a world unlike the one we experience. We hunger for a purpose or fulfillment that eludes us. Most of all, and related to all these aspects of our nature, we have a divine spiritual inner self that reflects God's own nature and connects to him and the world beyond the current form of earth.

Interestingly, Genesis 2 tells us that it is only when these two parts come together that we become human. A human is a clay vessel which contains the priceless Spirit of God. When God blows his breath (spirit) into our earthen bodies, we become "living souls." One way to describe our bodies, then, is little temples created to house a reflection of God's Spirit.

But we are getting ahead of ourselves. We need to read Genesis 1:26-31, 2:4-7 (NIV).

> Then God said, "Let us make mankind in our image, in our likeness, so that they may rule over the fish in the sea and the birds in the sky, over the livestock and all the wild animals, and over all the creatures that move along the ground."
> So God created mankind in his own image,
>   in the image of God he created them;
>   male and female he created them.
> God blessed them and said to them, "Be fruitful and increase in number; fill the earth and subdue it. Rule over the fish in the sea and the birds in the sky and over every living creature that moves on the ground."
> Then God said, "I give you every seed-bearing plant on the face of the whole earth and every tree that has fruit with seed in it. They will be yours for food. And to all the beasts of the earth and

all the birds in the sky and all the creatures that move along the ground—everything that has the breath of life in it—I give every green plant for food." And it was so.

God saw all that he had made, and it was very good. And there was evening, and there was morning—the sixth day.

This is the account of the heavens and the earth when they were created, when the Lord God made the earth and the heavens. Now no shrub had yet appeared on the earth and no plant had yet sprung up, for the Lord God had not sent rain on the earth and there was no one to work the ground, but streams came up from the earth and watered the whole surface of the ground. Then the Lord God formed a man from the dust of the ground and breathed into his nostrils the breath of life, and the man became a living being.

What does it mean to be made in the image and likeness of God? In the ancient world, it was common for rulers of large kingdoms or emperors, whose reign extended well beyond their immediate territory, where their subjects could not see them in person, to set up statues or images of themselves to remind people of exactly who ruled over them and their lands. These likenesses of the king were icons, and this is the same concept used in the creation narratives.

According to Genesis, humans are God's walking icons over creation. Like the animals we are dirt creatures who walk the "earth" (dust of the ground). But God inspires us, literally blows his Spirit (breath, wind) into our earthen bodies, to make us living icons that both represent him and extend his rule over the rest of creation. And when God makes us, he says we are good. We are like him. We are creatures with temporal bodies uniquely filled with a living spirit with the capacity for endless life that shares God's divine spark. He made us to reign over the earth with him and for him. As long as we are living in trusting intimacy with God, this is all good and right. While we are not gods, God's reality is demonstrated through us. We were not all powerful, but we were not flawed and had no reason to feel shame.

Think about how amazing this is and how it distinguishes humans from every form of life. Before there was original sin there was original blessing. Before there was a fall into evil, there was a profound goodness. **To be human is a remarkably good and beautiful thing. "Human" does not equal evil or broken.** Sin distorted us and left us sub-human. It was sin that caused us to lose the ability to house God's Spirit. We lost our intimacy with God. We lost our intended identity. But sin does not define our humanity. It is a departure from our created identity and purpose which Jesus came to restore. What we really long for is to recover our humanity.

That doesn't mean humanity was ever equal to divinity. We were always limited creatures with limited knowledge, power, and dominion. We were created to reflect God's goodness. We were never intended to function on our own. **Still, humanity is not defined by what is wrong with us, but by what is right about us.**

Is this how you think about yourself? You were created to be a glorious creature that reflects the glory of God. There is nothing wrong or evil about us being hybrid creatures composed of dirt and spirit. There is no shame in being human. There is no need to shed our bodies to be good. Our bodies need to be restored not abandoned. Jesus was not ashamed to take on a body, so why should we be? His resurrected body even carries the scars of his resurrection, and yet it is perfect and glorious. There is no reason for us to carry shame for having bodies, even bodies with scars.

True, sin distorted human nature and got embedded in our bodies like our minds. But our bodies are not more evil by nature than our minds, hearts, or spirits. That is why we should not be uncomfortable with our bodies. They were made to be good, and they play an important role in salvation and what is to come when all is restored.

I know this is not well understood in much of western Christianity, but it is all over our Bibles. Check out the following passages (NIV):

1 Corinthians 15:42-49

> So will it be with the resurrection of the dead. The body that is sown is perishable, it is raised imperishable; it is sown in dishonor, it is raised in glory; it is sown in weakness, it is raised in power; it is sown a natural body, it is raised a spiritual body.
>
> If there is a natural body, there is also a spiritual body. So it is written: "The first man Adam became a living being;" the last Adam, a life-giving spirit. The spiritual did not come first, but the

36

natural, and after that the spiritual. The first man was of the dust of the earth; the second man is of heaven. As was the earthly man, so are those who are of the earth; and as is the heavenly man, so also are those who are of heaven. And just as we have borne the image of the earthly man, so shall we bear the image of the heavenly man.
2 Corinthians 3:18

And we all, who with unveiled faces contemplate the Lord's glory, are being transformed into his image with ever-increasing glory, which comes from the Lord, who is the Spirit.

Colossians 1:15-20, 27, 3:10

The Son is the image of the invisible God, the firstborn over all creation. For in him all things were created: things in heaven and on earth, visible and invisible, whether thrones or powers or rulers or authorities; all things have been created through him and for him. He is before all things, and in him all things hold together. And he is the head of the body, the church; he is the beginning and the firstborn from among the dead, so that in everything he might have the supremacy. For God was pleased to have all his fullness dwell in him, and through him to reconcile to himself all things, whether things on earth or things in heaven, by making peace through his blood, shed on the cross.

To them God has chosen to make known among the Gentiles the glorious riches of this mystery, which is Christ in you, the hope of glory.

. . . and have put on the new self, which is being renewed in knowledge in the image of its Creator.

Notice that the goal of the Christian is never to get rid of our bodies so we can be pure spirit creatures. Rather, the goal is the resurrection of the body, restoration of God's marred image, and the restoration of God's Spirit in us. Jesus came in a body and was resurrected in a real physical body. He is the prototype of what all saved people will be. There is no disembodied salvation and that means the earth (meaning some place for saved bodies to live) has to be saved, renewed, or restored also (although what this actually entails is beyond our ability to comprehend or predict).

This is precisely what Paul says will happen in Romans 8:18-23 (NIV)

> I consider that our present sufferings are not worth comparing with the glory that will be revealed in us. For the creation waits in eager expectation for the children of God to be revealed. For the creation was subjected to frustration, not by its own choice, but by the will of the one who subjected it, in hope that the creation itself will be liberated from its bondage to decay and brought into the freedom and glory of the children of God.
>
> We know that the whole creation has been groaning as in the pains of childbirth right up to the present time. Not only so, but we ourselves, who have the firstfruits of the Spirit, groan inwardly as we wait eagerly for our adoption to sonship, the redemption of our bodies.

While there is still much here that we can't know, it is clear that salvation is not just about some spirit existence in a world-less afterlife; it is about all of life here and beyond. It is about who we are becoming now, not just where we end up. Jesus did not come to restore our divinity, i.e. turn us into angels (celestial beings); he came to restore our humanity and remake us in his image. Jesus came as the perfect human to show us what humanity was always supposed to be, what it can now be in him. Christ is the prototype of fully realized humanity and the first fruits of what all humanity will be in the age to come. He is the second Adam who begins a new race of redeemed and restored people (for more on this subject, read Romans 5:12-19, 1 Cor. 15:45-49).

Shocking as it may sound, this means that the goal of the Christian isn't to go to heaven; it is to be re-made in the full likeness and image of God now revealed in Jesus. Heaven is the reward, not the goal. The mission of the church is not to get the lost into church or

38

heaven per se, but to get Christ in the lost, and get the lost into all Christ is and is doing. Salvation isn't about going to a bodiless spirit-world; it is about overcoming our broken natures, which were created in God's image, but became much less. Salvation is being set free from sin, and being restored into the image of Jesus, whose life in us is eternal in nature. We begin to enjoy this eternal life now and will one day be able to enjoy it in its fullness in our eternal home described as a new heaven and new earth.

What this entails is hard for us to grasp. The "new earth" is not a slightly improved version of this earth. It will involve something cataclysmic, but whatever it will be, it is to be a place for our resurrected bodies. The earth we know will be profoundly changed, as will all of creation, but "heaven" involves a place, not just a consciousness. It is not about going back to Eden, as wonderful as that was. Eden was the infancy stage of what the restored earth will be when it reaches full maturity. What is coming will be better than Eden!

What does all this mean for us today? Among other things, it means that when people surrender their lives to Christ, he gets in them now. He draws them into his life, story, and people and begins to multiply that life outward through the concentric circles of their world. If Jesus gets into people, his life in them is eternal in quality and quantity. But the point isn't how long Jesus' life in us lasts, but the quality of Jesus' life, which starts now and grows into fullness only when all things are set right at the end (beyond this present age). **Without transformation into the image of Jesus, living forever would be a horrible curse, not a blessing**. The point isn't living forever but living on a different level. It is moving from mere existence to real life.

Eternal life (salvation) also means becoming part of a restored community. Disciples always require community and form new communities, but this is not the same thing as joining an institutional model of church. These two things are not opposed to each other or unrelated, but they are not the same thing.

Sadly, churches are filled with "members" who are not even trying to be disciples. We have often discounted Jesus' humanity and focused on his divinity because, on some level, we were seeking to avoid the expectation that we should become like Jesus in this life. If we can relegate salvation to an afterlife experience, we can lower the expectations this creates for our lives now. It is a subtle move with profound implications. It allows us to avoid pursuing spiritual maturity, righteousness, and justice.

In addition, if we don't understand grace and the role of the Spirit in empowering life in Jesus, the concept of discipleship, or becoming Christ-like, seems like an unrealistic burden. For those who understand the gospel, discipleship is quite the opposite. It is a liberation from slavery to oppressive forces of evil. It is a move from death into a life of grace upon grace as we increasingly let go of what is killing us for what can truly give us life.

Unfortunately, western Christianity has neglected the resurrection for so long that we almost don't notice how it leaves us empty and always searching for something else. We satisfied ourselves with an afterlife only salvation, which left us in the mess of a life we have now. We don't talk much about having a resurrected body in a "new heaven and new earth" like Jesus' resurrected body. We have not explored the implications of Jesus as the second Adam who restores our humanity and sets us on a new path in this life and the life beyond this.

The New Testament is consistent in telling us that Jesus came to restore our humanity, i.e., to repair us so our bodies can contain the Spirit and nature of God. He came to restore the image of God in us. If the goal is just to go to a spirit heaven, all that matters is making sure we've met the requirements. Ultimately, then, it is impossible to avoid legalism. We may set a high standard or low standard for what we have to do to be saved, but it is still about "qualifying" so we "get in." But, what about growing in Christ? What about sanctification? If all that matters is getting in, these things become optional or irrelevant.

However, if the goal is to become like Jesus (i.e., have our humanity restored), we embark on a lifelong process of maturation and development that ultimately ends with life in God's presence with Jesus. First, Christ gets into us. But, because his life is so much grander than ours, the goal is not just to have him in us. It is better to say we get into his life. The whole idea of inviting Jesus into our life has a certain appeal, but it makes us the object, which is rather silly. Instead of just coming into our life, Jesus draws us into his fullness as we seek to grow toward fullness in Christ. It is the fulfillment of a lifelong project that is a matter of faith and grace from first to last (Romans 1:17).

We can't become like Christ on our own--it requires his work on us by his Spirit in his community called church, and all we contribute is submission. Submission is not about God's ego needing affirmation or his being a control freak. Rather, submission is about God's creatures joining—instead of obstructing—his purpose on earth. It is about us learning to dance to his music so that all of creation works together harmoniously again. Once we understand what salvation really means, any notion of merit becomes properly laughable. It is grace or nothing.

When I was 19, I moved to Houston to be part of a Bible school that met in the evenings. This school was started to train ministers, and it still had a track for ordination at that time. But mostly it was a discipleship school. What I learned in being part of that community is that being formed in the ways of Jesus may be supported by Bible teaching, but it is really empowered by a rich community life of people who share a common passion and way of life. I felt more alive than I could have imagined previously, and I had grown up deeply involved in church. While I came to view any number of issues differently than the positions our teachers gave us in the mid-80's at this small school, the impact of the community life and the way God's Spirit drew me into fuller life has stayed with me always and left me longing for that kind of community ever since.

When we get clarity about salvation being a restoration of our humanity that starts now and carries on until the restoration of all things, it changes how we see our mission. We are inviting other people into a real life, not just an afterlife. If the church is offering help for this life instead of just tickets to the afterlife, we will need to get in the dirt with people and model what it means to be the Spirit-filled presence of God in every aspect of life, even the most mundane. No part of life or humanity is outside God's interest and transforming power.

This also should change our church "programs." Instead of just asking people to leave "daily life" and the "things of this world," we will prepare people to take Jesus into daily life and the things of this world as God's image-bearers. The church is not an escape from this world, but a community of people who live out God's presence in the world. Worship and ministry gatherings should remind us of who we are and prepare us to engage the world in new and fresh ways. Ministry happens "out there." Worship services are somewhat like halftime meetings where we focus on our coach and get prepared to go back out on the field to play the game. We need to be asking, "How can we take our ministries outside the building and into the world?"

This refined understanding of salvation also changes our definition of ministry success. Instead of being concerned about how many people gather, we can be concerned about preparing them for what they do when they scatter, and how many of them are equipped to live on mission as God's image-bearers. Instead of counting how many people will be "going to heaven when they die," we should be counting how many are carrying heaven into the world while they live. We don't just ask people, "What would happen to you if you died tonight?" Instead we are asking them to ponder, "How am I doing in growing into God's image? How can I give God greater access to transform me?"

What do you do with all this change of perspective? First, pray. **Pray for God to give you peace with your body and all that goes with being a physical creature**. Pray that God will inhabit and redeem every aspect of your body and life so that his glory can be revealed in you. Pray that God will show you how you can represent him to people near you who don't know him by being his presence among them. Ask God to give you the names of those people and show you how to be Christ to them.

Then go. Find a place or two in the world to engage. Almost any place will do. But go out, serve people, earn their trust. Be good news. Then tell good news.

Putting this into practice

One way to think about acting out the gospel is by putting it in this form: Incarnation, Crucifixion, Resurrection, Ascension.

- Incarnation means physically entering in the world of those you want to reach.
- Crucifixion means being willing to suffer loss or pay a price to reach others.
- Resurrection means we trust God to raise up new life.
- Ascension means that we "leave" and trust. We don't try to stay and control what God raises up.

42

What is an incarnational step you can take?

1. Where is there a community near you that you can begin to spend time in and form relationships with people far from God?
2. What price will it cost you to be there often enough to make an impact?

Chapter 5:

Mission #2: Restoration of All Creation
Why Seeking the Wrong Heaven Is Damning the Earth

I'm a big fan of The Far Side cartoons and think Gary Larson is a genius. I used to get a Far Side calendar every year for Christmas and I grieve that Larson quit producing the cartoon series. Many of my favorite cartoons were spoofs of the cultural concepts of heaven and hell.

In one cartoon, a devil is escorting a classical symphony conductor to his cell in "Hell" and it was filled with guys playing banjos. In another, there is a guy in "Heaven" with wings, in a robe, sitting on a cloud by himself, and he is thinking, "I wish I'd brought a magazine."

Now, I know that real heaven and hell are no laughing matter, but the ways many people in the western world think about them is. Our pictures of the end times are often so distorted that there is not much we can do except laugh and re-examine what the Bible really says. Sadly, our failure to grasp and proclaim an accurate picture of the end of all things that is in keeping with scripture has kept many people from taking the gospel seriously.

In the last chapter, I wrote about how confused we can get by the talk of people "getting saved." I suggested that salvation is not really about the afterlife, or at least not limited to the afterlife. If that surprises you, I'd encourage you to consider whether Jesus ever spoke about "going to heaven when we die?" Is that language in the Bible? If so, where? Heaven shows up for sure, but not in the way we typically talk about it in Western culture, or even in church much of the time.

For many years, the church in the Western world has been confused about what God is doing and what salvation is really about. We got the idea that salvation was about escaping the physical world for a spirit world called heaven. But if that were true, why would we need a resurrection of the body? Why would scripture talk about a "new earth?" Remember, God created the physical world to be a good place and he wants to restore it, not destroy it.

One of the best places to see this in scripture is Acts 3. While you really need to read the whole story to get the context, I want us to focus on Acts 3:17-21 (NIV):

> "Now, fellow Israelites, I know that you acted in ignorance, as did your leaders. But this is how God fulfilled what he had foretold through all the prophets, saying that his Messiah would suffer. Repent, then, and turn to God, so that your sins may be wiped out, that times of refreshing may come from the Lord, and that he may send the Messiah, who has been appointed for you—even Jesus. Heaven must receive him until the time comes for God to restore everything, as he promised long ago through his holy prophets.

When Peter describes what God is doing through Jesus, he lists three related items: forgiveness of sins, times of refreshing from the Lord, and the coming "restoring of all things." Notice he does not talk about the destruction of all things, but the restoration of all things. This does not present a picture of the elimination of the creation, but the purification of the creation. In this story, the coming restoration is demonstrated in the miracle that sparks Peter's sermon. The healing of the crippled beggar was not just a display of power, or an attention-getting warm up for a sermon. It was a preview of what is coming when Jesus' reign comes in full.

Probably the best place to see what this means is Romans 8:18-25 (NIV)

> I consider that our present sufferings are not worth comparing with the glory that will be revealed in us. For the creation waits in eager expectation for the children of God to be revealed. For the creation was subjected to frustration, not by its own choice, but by the will of the one who subjected it, in hope that the creation itself will be liberated from its bondage to decay and brought into the freedom and glory of the children of God.

We know that the whole creation has been groaning as in the pains of childbirth right up to the present time. Not only so, but we ourselves, who have the firstfruits of the Spirit, groan inwardly as we wait eagerly for our adoption to sonship, the redemption of our bodies. For in this hope we were saved. But hope that is seen is no hope at all. Who hopes for what they already have? But if we hope for what we do not yet have, we wait for it patiently.

Notice how big the coming salvation is and what all will be impacted. It is not only human souls who will be saved, but all creation will be "set free from its bondage to corruption" and "obtain the freedom of the glory of the children of God." **The earth is not going to be thrown in the cosmic waste dump, but liberated from the curse of sin, purified of all corruption, and restored to a perfected form**. Since God created the physical world and declared it is good, he is not willing to let the evil one and sin ruin it forever. He is going to restore all things and restore humanity's created place in creation.

Now does that mean we will live on the earth as we know it now? No. It will change vastly. These things are beyond our current comprehension and trying to grasp them beyond the images given to us will probably lead us to as much confusion as clarity. There is no way to know precisely what that perfected world will be like, but it won't be limited to what we know or even what we can imagine now. Whatever it is, it will not be the end of space, physical places, and bodies. We will not end up in some disembodied consciousness. "Heaven" (or new heaven and new earth) is the expansion, fulfillment, and perfection of the creation, not its end.

When we understand this, Jesus' miracles make more sense. They were not publicity stunts. Instead they were sneak peaks of the coming restored heaven and earth where all is to be set right. **Jesus' acts of healing, exorcism of evil spirits, control of nature, and restoration of alienated people to society were not just magic tricks to get people's attention so he could then tell them how to go to heaven. They were examples of the restoring (saving) power of the gospel which involves setting all things right again.**

Doesn't a renewed creation have more appeal to you than going to some ethereal spirit heaven? It certainly does to me. Who wants to be a free-floating spirit or play a harp on a cloud forever? I'd need more than a magazine to keep me from feeling like this was a form of punishment. But the idea of perfected, resurrected bodies with boundless energy and unresisted stewardship over creation, bodies that can walk on water, control the weather, and turn water to wine? That sounds awesome!

As we discussed in the last chapter, Christians in our culture have a hard time accepting our bodies as good things because we confuse them with our sinful nature. Some of this has a long history in Greek philosophy, and some of it has been complicated by the KJV's translations of passages like Romans 7:18, 25 where Paul refers to the broken part of us as "flesh." But Paul wasn't talking about our bodies being bad. He was saying that an evil force has taken up residence in our bodies and has contaminated them. This force distorts our bodies and turns them against God's purpose for us. Our bodies are good by nature and will be restored in the resurrection, like Jesus' resurrected body. The biblical vision of salvation is not to escape our bodies, but to have our bodies transformed and perfected so they belong in the restored heaven and earth (cf. all of 1 Corinthians 15).

Paul's choice of the Greek word *sarx* (translated "flesh" in the KJV) to describe our sinful natures (rebellious spirit or brokenness) made it easy to confuse our bodies with our sin nature. But Paul did not say our bodies (Gk *soma*) were the problem, but that something else, which easily resides in our bodies, distorts, and contaminates them. **If we think our core problem is having bodies, we will view salvation as escaping our bodies, and heaven then becomes a non-material spiritual state**. This may explain why gluttony is rampant among Christians in America. We just see the evil in abusing our bodies. The goal then seems to be escaping our humanity and any kind of earth with a heaven (sky) for some angelic spirit world with God. But a disembodied spirit world is hard to get excited about and doesn't seem like good news to most people because we were created to be physical creatures and can't really imagine life without bodies of some sort. Our deepest longings, as designed by God, are for a perfected world and perfected bodies, not an escape from our bodies for some immaterial world.

All this means that your body is a good thing created by God, not something to be ashamed of. The harsh division between the spiritual and material universe, which goes back at least 500 years before Christ to Plato, is a major problem that has confused Christian thinking from the second century on. It needs to be confronted as dangerous heresy. Our problem is not that we are physical creatures but that we are sinful creatures. Our problem is not that we have bodies that we need to escape, but that we have wills that don't want to submit to God's reign. Heaven is where God's will is done now. One day, earth will be where God's will is done also. That is Jesus' prayer and God will answer it.

The New Testament pictures salvation as a new heaven (or heavens—meaning sky, space, and the dwelling place of God) and earth. Read 2 Peter 3:13 (NIV):

> But in keeping with his promise we are looking forward to a new heaven and a new earth, where righteousness dwells.

and Revelation 21:1-4 (NIV):

> Then I saw "a new heaven and a new earth," for the first heaven and the first earth had passed away, and there was no longer any sea. I saw the Holy City, the new Jerusalem, coming down out of heaven from God, prepared as a bride beautifully dressed for her husband. And I heard a loud voice from the throne saying, "Look! God's dwelling place is now among the people, and he will dwell with them. They will be his people, and God himself will be with them and be their God. 'He will wipe every tear from their eyes. There will be no more death' or mourning or crying or pain, for the old order of things has passed away."

Instead of being destroyed and removed, the earth and the heavens will be refined and restored to be suitable environments for the redeemed to live in their resurrected bodies. God promises to come down to live with us in a renewed earth—a renewed Eden for the new descendants of the 2nd Adam. In the epic vision of Revelation 21-22, this is described as a remarriage between God and all his creation, and all the nations of the world will bring their treasures into the perfected world to come.

The Christian hope is not for the destruction of the material universe and escape to a pure spirit heaven, but a purification process that will leave us with new heavens and a new earth, which we will inhabit with perfect resurrection bodies. Because God is not seeking to destroy the earth, matter matters. Our bodies were intended to be temples to house God's Spirit, which gets restored in Jesus. Salvation is not just escaping this world after death, but experiencing transformation in our bodies, families, communities, and world now, as previews of the final salvation. The whole creation is to be saved and restored, and the church is to be a sign, foretaste, and instrument of this salvation now. Therefore, caring about creation now, dealing right now with people's physical, emotional, and social worlds, and working for the totality of life, are all part of salvation.

If we understood that God loves not only our bodies but all creation, it would also make a big difference in how we take care of both. We would likely develop an enhanced purpose to care for our bodies as the temples of God if we understood these bodies are good things God can inhabit and plans to resurrect and perfect. What do you need to do to care for your temple? We would also likely do a better job of caring for the earth if we remembered that we are only stewards of this planet, and that God doesn't plan to throw it away but restore it.

The implications of a better understanding of the new heaven and earth are far reaching. It changes how we present the gospel to people. It changes how we live out the gospel in our city. Our ministries should include elements that give people a preview of what is coming in God's future completed salvation. This changes how we think about our physical space (homes, yards, farms, and church facilities as well as cities and general environment). How cities are laid out, how neighborhoods are planned, public transportation, mining, energy, and agriculture are all impacted by how we view the purpose and end of God's creation. Everything we see and all we do should take on and reflect the concept of redeemed and holy space where God reigns.

The OT prophets often described how the sin of the world hurt the earth. The creation pays the price for our sins and longs to be redeemed and restored. When we are living as caretakers of God's creation, we will treat it with honor and preserve and perfect it. When we lose this sense and look for a spirit-only heaven, we lose touch with our role as caretakers of creation and the earth pays an increasing price. How odd it is that people who claim to take the Bible seriously are often unconcerned about matters of the environment. Of all people, we should be most concerned to care for the world God has placed in our care. We should value physical space and want it all to reflect God's glory and goodness. We believe it is going to be with us forever. God is already working through his people to redeem and restore his world. That may put priority on creatures made in his image, but it also includes the world they inhabit. There are no secular places. There are only sacred and desecrated places.[14] God wants it all back.

In addition, we can't love people or offer them salvation if we won't get into their physical world and help them with the many ways sin or brokenness (rebellion to God's reign/Kingdom) have harmed them. The church is called to be a demonstration that a new kind of life is possible in a significant way now, not unlike what God wanted from Israel when he set them as a model before the nations of the ancient world. **The church is commissioned to give people hope that a total transformation is coming. We are the preview of the coming attraction.** We are not intended merely to be arks in which people ride out the flood. The church is called to live out as much of a redeemed experience as possible in a fallen world by the power of God's Spirit in us. That means we have to engage all of life as creatures in a beautiful but broken world. **Every part of life needs to come under the reign of God and the transforming power of the gospel.**

Putting this into practice

---

[14] Breathe with unconditional breath
the unconditioned air.
Shun electric wire.
Communicate slowly. Live
a three-dimensioned life;
stay away from screens.
Stay away from anything
that obscures the place it is in.
There are no unsacred places;
there are only sacred places
and desecrated places.
Wendell Berry, "How to Be a Poet"

1. Develop a plan to care for your body as the temple of God.
2. Consider starting a garden or committing to get out in nature every week. Doing your own yard work and putting time and money into cultivating beauty on the land is a powerful spiritual practice.
3. Work with your neighborhood or city to create green spaces and renewable energy.
4. Create a holy space or thin space in or near your home where you pray.

Chapter 6:

The Mission Embarks: The Call of Abraham
The Gospel Didn't Start in the Gospels

As I write this, I've been married for 32 years. That is, by far, the majority of my life. My relationship with my wife began before our marriage, but we celebrate the anniversary of our wedding day, not the day we met, went on our first date, knew we were in love, or got engaged. Why? Why do we count wedding anniversaries and celebrate that date instead of celebrating when our relationship began? Weddings can be hard to remember. My wedding day was so hectic it has become something of a blur. It rarely comes to my mind when I think about the development of my relationship with my wife. Yet this is the day we celebrate each year.

How many people start telling the story of their marriage with their wedding? Weddings change a relationship, but they don't create it. What happens at a wedding matters profoundly, but only because it marks a major transition in a relationship, not because it begins it (at least in western countries). How the marriage goes is often established well before that day. How something begins really matters, and it shapes the rest of the story.

When did the story we call good news or gospel begin? It's hard to pin down a date. We could make an argument for Jesus' birth being the start. Two of our Gospels start there . . . almost. But even Matthew and Luke, who have birth narratives, have to tell us some pieces of the backstory to Jesus' birth. We could make a good case that the gospel began when Jesus rose from the tomb. Something changed and new hope emerged. But that is the end of the "Gospels," not the beginning of the story.

We could argue, as some from my fellowship have, that the gospel really was launched on the day of Pentecost, recorded in Acts 2. On that day Peter preached the first "gospel" sermon and 3,000 people became disciples. That is the church's birthday in a way. But, again, Acts is the second chapter in book two of a set of books written by Luke. Both books are rooted in a much older story that Luke constantly

53

references, by allusion if not always overt quotes, to make sense of his account of God's work in Jesus and Jesus' followers.

While you could make a case for all these answers, perhaps the best answer to the question of when the Gospel began is Genesis 12 with the call of Abraham (or Abram before his call). The story of God's mission certainly reaches a climax in Jesus and his resurrection from the dead, and it goes public in a bold way on Pentecost, but it begins when God selects and commissions a family to work through to save God's world. Genesis 1-3 tell of creation and the entrance of sin into the world. Genesis 4-11 demonstrate the futility of a top-down salvation strategy, like the flood. Then in chapter 12, God introduces an incremental approach of restoring his world that unfolds over time. It starts with one couple, expanding to one family/tribe, 12 tribes, one nation, and then the whole world. But the whole world was always in God's mind even when that was not so clear in the story. That is an essential aspect of the story and it shapes how we understand it and live it out to this day.

To fully comprehend it, we need to back up a little. After Adam and Eve rebelled and were driven from the garden and tree of life, humanity spiraled out of control and nothing seemed able to stop them. Cain killed Abel in fear and jealousy. The first big brother killed his first little brother, and so began the pattern of the righteous being slaughtered by the jealous and corrupt of heart. Soon, that became the norm. The righteous few were overrun and eliminated by the wicked. The line of this evil grew and became increasingly out of touch with God. What started out as a "very good" world soon looked hopeless. Things got so bad that God determined to wipe out all of humanity and start over with one good family in the flood.

Sadly, even that extreme level of judgment and punishment didn't fix the problem of sin. **The flood demonstrates that sin can't be solved with punishment. No amount of condemnation, no punishment is harsh enough to solve the human sin problem**. Only after proving that we can't save the world through acts of judgement did God show us how to save a world through grace and love, a little at a time, like a mustard seed.

Before we go any farther, we need to read Genesis 11:27-12:20 (NIV):

54

This is the account of Terah's family line. Terah became the father of Abram, Nahor and Haran. And Haran became the father of Lot. While his father Terah was still alive, Haran died in Ur of the Chaldeans, in the land of his birth. Abram and Nahor both married. The name of Abram's wife was Sarai

This is the account of Terah's family line. Terah became the father of Abram, Nahor and Haran. And Haran became the father of Lot. While his father Terah was still alive, Haran died in Ur of the Chaldeans, in the land of his birth. Abram and Nahor both married. The name of Abram's wife was Sarai, and the name of Nahor's wife was Milkah; she was the daughter of Haran, the father of both Milkah and Iskah. Now Sarai was childless because she was not able to conceive.

Terah took his son Abram, his grandson Lot son of Haran, and his daughter-in-law Sarai, the wife of his son Abram, and together they set out from Ur of the Chaldeansto go to Canaan. But when they came to Harran, they settled there.

Terah lived 205 years, and he died in Harran.

The Lord had said to Abram, "Go from your country, your people and your   father's household to the land I will show you.

> "I will make you into a great nation,
>   and I will bless you;
> I will make your name great,
>   and you will be a blessing.[a]
> I will bless those who bless you,
>   and whoever curses you I will curse;
> and all peoples on earth
>   will be blessed through you."

So Abram went, as the Lord had told him; and Lot went with him. Abram was seventy-five years old when he set out from Harran. He took his wife Sarai, his nephew Lot, all the possessions they had accumulated and the people they had acquired in Harran, and they set out for the land of Canaan, and they arrived there.

Abram traveled through the land as far as the site of the great tree of Moreh at Shechem. At that time the Canaanites were in the land. The Lord appeared to Abram and said, "To your offspring I will give this land." So he built an altar there to the Lord, who had appeared to him. From there he went on toward the hills east of Bethel and pitched his tent, with Bethel on the west and Ai on the east. There he built an altar to the Lord and called on the name of the Lord.

Then Abram set out and continued toward the Negev.

Now there was a famine in the land, and Abram went down to Egypt to live there for a while because the famine was severe. As he was about to enter Egypt, he said to his wife Sarai, "I know what a beautiful woman you are. When the Egyptians see you, they will say, 'This is his wife.' Then they will kill me but will let you live. Say you are my sister, so that I will be treated well for your sake and my life will be spared because of you."

When Abram came to Egypt, the Egyptians saw that Sarai was a very beautiful woman. And when Pharaoh's officials saw her, they praised her to Pharaoh, and she was taken into his palace. He treated Abram well for her sake, and Abram acquired sheep and cattle, male and female donkeys, male and female servants, and camels.

But the Lord inflicted serious diseases on Pharaoh and his household because of Abram's wife Sarai. So, Pharaoh summoned Abram. "What have you done to me?" he said. "Why didn't you tell me she was your wife? Why did you say, 'She is my sister,' so that I took her to be my wife? Now then, here is your wife. Take her and go!" Then Pharaoh gave orders about Abram to his men, and they sent him on his way, with his wife and everything he had.

This story does not seem to be as important as it turns out to be later. It just seems like one little episode in the life of some new character from some obscure location in antiquity. No one of real

56

power in that day would have been aware or impacted by Abraham or his call from God. Only one family knew about it, and perhaps only Abraham really knew what had happened.

Abraham was a nobody who had done nothing. He was a wandering immigrant with no clear plan or purpose who was living out a strange calling from an unknown god (in a culture where he knew of many gods) to go to an unknown place for murky reasons. But go he did. It is hard for us to look past the legendary status Abraham (his later name) acquires in the full biblical narrative to see who Abram was at the beginning. Abram was a no one. He had done nothing to distinguish himself in order to receive this call.

Perhaps Abraham was a man of outstanding virtue like Noah, but that is never said in scripture. No virtue of Abraham before his call is listed. In fact, one of the first things he does in the story is leave the promised land in fear and lie about his wife's identity to protect himself. Whatever made God choose Abraham, it wasn't his flawless character.

So, what distinguished Abraham from everyone else? Only this—he went when he was called. That's it. Do you think it possible that God called several people and Abraham was the only one who obeyed? It is even possible that Abraham's father, Terah, got the call but didn't follow through. That would make some sense of why Terah set out with his family for Canaan but stopped short in Haran.

Speculation aside, what Abraham did was odd, but it is still impressive. He launched into uncertainty based on a vision. He couldn't Google Canaan and prepare for what was coming. He didn't even know what place to research, had there even been a way to do that. He didn't have a map or compass. He left his country, culture, people, language, and family to become an immigrant in a strange land. That means he had no protection from a tribe or nation in a violent world of warlords. He was vulnerable with nothing but his new God to protect him. What kind of life is that? A very insecure one, unless this new God turns out to be more powerful than any god of Mesopotamia. No one had heard of a universal creator God back home. All gods were local and limited. Abraham was a bold maverick, because he chose to believe the God who appeared to him could be bigger than one people and one place.

For that amazing trust, God made equally amazing promises to Abraham. He promised to make Abraham into a great nation. God will bless him and give him a legendary name. God will base how he treats all other people groups by how they treat Abraham. Bless Abraham and be blessed by God. Curse Abraham and be cursed by God. God promised to make Abraham the fulcrum of history. All things for all people groups will hinge on what God is starting with Abraham. This is as big as the whole earth and will last longer than the civilizations of ancient Samaria, Egypt, or any other subsequent empire. It doesn't look like much of a start. It wouldn't make the evening news. It was as obscure as a teenage mother giving birth in a barn in Bethlehem centuries later, but the world changed when Abraham loaded his U-Haul camels and pulled out.

But lest we wax poetic and turn Abraham into a legend instead of a person, the next story shows us his faith has gaps. This story won't run in a straight line. It will go in fits and starts. No sooner does Abraham obey and worship his new God in the promised land than he gets scared and leaves it. He thinks Egypt looks more secure and doesn't trust the God who called him to protect him and starts trusting deceit and diplomacy instead of God's promise. He lies about Sarah (Sarai at the time) to save himself.

But God keeps his promises even when Abraham doesn't fully trust him. And, the problems start for Egypt when Sarah ends up in Pharaoh's haram. Abraham is crucial to Egypt's future even when Abraham doubts God and is less than honorable. God does not give up on Abraham or expect him to be born full grown. His faith is new and his performance will vary. He is not God's servant by virtue of his excellence but by God's grace. God will shape him and grow him into the man he needs him to be. We can watch him display amazing faith and fail in predictable patterns in the episodes to come. That same pattern will be displayed in Abraham's family and the nation that grows from them. Yet, God will not let them go. He is determined to do what he set out to do through this family because he has a massive plan in place to save the world. Nothing is going to deter him, not even the weaknesses of his chosen people.

It is quite remarkable how God treats Abraham as his partner in world events. Before he decides to eliminate some intolerable wicked cities, whose corruption is too great to allow the world to be put at risk from their influence, God informs and draws Abraham into his counsel in Genesis 18. Abraham even helps God determine the threshold for judgement. The fate of these people is being impacted by Abraham's relationship with God. Why? Here is what is said in Genesis 18:16-19 (NIV):

> When the men got up to leave, they looked down toward Sodom, and Abraham walked along with them to see them on their way. Then the Lord said, "Shall I hide from Abraham what I am about to do? Abraham will surely become a great and powerful nation, and all nations on earth will be blessed through him. For I have chosen him, so that he will direct his children and his household after him to keep the way of the Lord by doing what is right and just, so that the Lord will bring about for Abraham what he has promised him."

Because, the salvation of the world flows through this man and his family. He will be the one who fathers a unique people through whom God will save the world. He is not just the "exalted father" (which is what Abram means) but the "father of many" nations (which is what Abraham means) whom God will call (cf. Galatians 3:29-4:7), even those who have no biological heritage from him. He represents a new way of being in this corrupted world—a way of faith and grace that can make us children of God—and restores the intimacy we lost in the Garden of Eden.

Just as Abraham's descendants carry on his mission, often with little understanding of their role in the story, the church continues the calling of Abraham in our day. The writer of Hebrews 11:13-16 says it well (NIV):

> All these people were still living by faith when they died. They did not receive the things promised; they only saw them and welcomed them from a distance, admitting that they were foreigners and strangers on earth. People who say such things show that they are looking for a country of their own. If they had been thinking of the country they had left, they would have had opportunity to return. Instead, they were longing for a better

country—a heavenly one. Therefore God is not ashamed to be called their God, for he has prepared a city for them.

Abraham's mentality should be our model today. Like him, we don't identify ourselves as citizens of whichever country issues us our passport or requires us to pay taxes. Our origin is in another land. We are all like immigrants or refugees of God's kingdom in the country where we live. This is not our true home, even if we have been here for generations. We are from another land. We are all looking to go "home" to a country of our own and a city that will descend from the clouds when all is set right. We should all be cultivating and keeping the same sense of calling, connection, and culture that Abraham modeled. We don't identify with our earthly country first. Not even close. We are Jesus' people more than we are Americans or citizens of any other country.

As Peter tells the early Christians in the land we now call Turkey (cf. 1 Peter 1:1-2, 2:9-12), our national and cultural identity as disciples of Jesus makes us undocumented aliens even in the land of our birth among those whose language we speak. That is hard for Christians in America, or another country with a strong Christian tradition, who often confuse our national and spiritual identity. It is not easy for us to decide if we are Christians in America or if we are American Christians. But it really matters which is most true. It dramatically determines how we live our lives. Our identity impacts our calling, mission, and interaction with our neighbors locally and globally.

The primary purpose of the "good lives" and "good deeds" which disciples are called to carry out is not to earn salvation or establish our identity as God's people. That is beyond us. But how we live does determine our mission. We are called to live in the ways of God, best reflected in Jesus, not merely for our benefit but for the glory of God and attraction of the nations (ethnic groups) around us. The life of Abraham's spiritual heirs puts the Kingdom of God culture on display and reveals there is another way that is really life and hope.

Just as Abraham was called for the sake of all the nations and not just for himself, his family, or the people of Israel that came from his descendants, the church is not called to serve only its members, but its neighborhood, city, nation, and world. What made Abraham special was God's call, not his virtue. The same is true for us. God called Abraham for the whole world, not just his family. God still calls the few for the sake of the many. As God's people, we do not exist to serve ourselves or protect ourselves from the world. We are here for the sake of the world.

We need to take note of our neighbors in our city. We need to track who God is bringing near us by immigration. We are called to all people, not just our nation or our race. How do we connect with those around us for the sake of God's mission? Just imagine, how would it change the church if we saw ourselves as the aliens and outsiders in our world, instead of the insiders who need to protect "our land" from "those people"?

Because salvation involves all of creation and humanity's entire life, God needed a model of what he was seeking from all nations in a specific people who could embody God's reign in a specific place on the earth. That story started with Abraham, but it wasn't about Abraham. It ran through Israel, but it wasn't about Israel. It is true for the church, but it isn't about the church.

Since God's goal isn't just to save disembodied souls in a spirit heaven but to restore all people and all creation, God needed to start with a prototype in a specific physical place and time. God began to reveal himself and his vision to one family, which became one nation, but his goal was always to bless "all nations" and draw them into his glorious future

Election by God is still for the sake of mission not status. The church is a people who exist for the glory and reign of God and salvation of the world. The lost are not raw material to build up the church. The church is God's instrument to rebuild and restore the world and all the nations. A sense of superiority or entitlement among God's people is deadly to our ability to accomplish our mission. We are set apart not because we are better, but because we are responsible to pass on what God has done among us.

Putting this into practice

Do some research and develop answers to the following questions:

1. Who are our neighbors in our city? Who is God bringing to the 5 zip codes closest to our church building or home?
2. How do we meet these people and begin forming relationships with them?
3. How would it change us if we saw ourselves as the aliens and outsiders in our country?
4. When are you most prone to feel like a resident alien in your own culture?
5. When is it most difficult for you to see yourself as an alien here?
6. How can you live out these understandings through the relationships you've been cultivating?

Chapter 7:

Big Salvation Story #1: The Exodus and Conquest
The God of Slaves and Refugees Who Takes Down Empires

In the U.S. presidential election of 2016, we all got a lesson on how much fear Americans feel toward refugees and immigrants in our age of rapid globalization. Immigration policy deeply shaped the outcome of the election and much of the political conversation in the subsequent years. But, this is not just an American issue. From Brexit in the UK to recent legislation proposed and accepted around Western Europe designed to protect the historic cultures of Europe from the influence of other cultures, we are seeing a common phenomenon of humanity: xenophobia.

This is completely understandable and predictable. It is the normal human condition to fear outsiders, who are seen as a threat to "us." Any time the majority population begins to sense that they are losing control of their culture in any country, you can expect a strong reaction. Us v. them thinking is the norm for humans everywhere. Welcoming the "other" has always been an exceptional mindset in a world filled with conflict and a legacy of warfare between people groups. This is part of what makes the gospel unique and compelling. But this is always what makes it hard to accept.

In addition, it is common for all people groups to assume we are the standard and all other cultures are inferior in some way. We assume the way we think is normal and that our culture is good. All other worldviews and ways of life seem strange or just plain wrong to us.

I remember as a child, I was always struck by how "weird" my friends' families where when I spent the night with them and ate in their homes. They would do bizarre things like putting ketchup on their scrambled eggs or skip the prayer before the meal. They just didn't do things the normal or correct way like my family. No one had to teach me this. I just assumed my family was the standard. Don't we all?

Not only do we assume that "we" are the standard, we also naturally seek our own advantage wherever we can. Every people group uses whatever power they have at their disposal to look after their own interests and protect themselves from the threats posed by outsiders. We live in a world of fear, competition, conflict, and oppression. These are all default traits in a fallen world. Even in a country built on immigration, like the United States, we find cultural diversity difficult because it is. America practices cultural diversity better than many nations, but we still find it extremely difficult.

When the United States has been at its best, we have lived out the words inscribed on the Statue of Liberty.

> *"Keep, ancient lands, your storied pomp!" cries she*
> *With silent lips. "Give me your tired, your poor,*
> *Your huddled masses yearning to breathe free,*
> *The wretched refuse of your teeming shore.*
> *Send these, the homeless, tempest-tossed to me,*
> *I lift my lamp beside the golden door!"*

As admirable as this mentality is, it has always been fragile, and even our nation of immigrants struggles to welcome those who show up after "our people" did.

This is true of Christians as well. Most American Christians are so deeply enmeshed in our national identity that we fail to see how these forces shape us and how out of step they are with the gospel. We know we are called to love all people and be compassionate on a personal level, but we struggle to make sense of these teachings on a societal level. The radical individualism of western Christianity has eclipsed the social aspects of the gospel. Our commitment to compassion gets overwhelmed when our fear of outsiders and foreigners comes to the surface. Reconciling our identity as members of God's kingdom and our national identities is extremely difficult. That is why Christians are all over the map when it comes to how we deal with issues like race, culture, immigration, and refugees.

If you ask a group of American Christians how they feel about refugees and immigrants, you will get a wide range of responses. Some will say, "They scare me. I want to help them, but not if it puts my life or family at risk." Others think, "I wish they would just go away. This country is for us." Others will point out that we are a nation of immigrants and welcome them with open arms without any serious consideration for national security. Others take a moderate perspective and say, "It depends on where they come from and why they are here. We need to be careful who we let in, so we don't put ourselves at risk." These are complex matters that elude simple answers.

Interestingly, Christians of the first century were treated like aliens and exiles in their world. Disciples of Jesus were seen as so odd that they frequently became objects of fear to the Roman culture. Yet, they were described in this way in by the anonymous Christian writer of the "Letter to Diognetus" V:

> They dwell in their own fatherlands but as if sojourners in them...Every foreign country is their fatherland and every fatherland a foreign country...They pass their time upon the earth but their citizenship is in heaven...

That is no longer the case in our context. Christians typically feel like insiders who demand "our rights" in "our country." We have engaged in "culture wars" for several decades because we think we are the legitimate heirs of our nation's story.

How does our identity and calling as God's people on mission in Jesus' name inform our relationship to our country and to people from other countries? Sadly, that question is not often summoned into the conversation because many western believers don't think it is relevant. We don't understand God's mission in a way that speaks to this issue. We really struggle to distinguish our national identity from our Christian identity.

No doubt, the world we live in is a scary place, and the fear of evil can turn us against people who are not "us." If we give in to this kind of fear, we will diminish what the gospel says about God's purpose in reconciling all nations. Our fallen human nature cannot be trusted to direct us in such matters, because it is concerned with self and "our people." This goes back to the beginning when our first parents turned away from a life of trust and vulnerability in the garden and began to look out for our own good by our own plans. **God's**

redemption of his people is comprehensive of all aspects of life. There are no issues outside the range of the gospel.

This is not hard to see if we will just reflect on the exodus story and what it reveals about who God is. This big OT salvation story lays out a paradigm for how God deals with other powers in the world.

In the middle of the Law of Moses, we find this rather striking quote from Leviticus 19:34 (NIV):

> "The foreigner residing among you must be treated as your native-born. Love them as yourself, for you were foreigners in Egypt. I am the Lord your God."

Given Israel's struggles with other nations and sense of unique importance to God, this is striking. It remains striking in every nation today. But this quote reflects how deeply embedded in Israel's story is the memory that they were once an oppressed immigrant minority in the empire of Egypt. Yet, despite Israel's oppression by Egypt, God had mercy on them and rescued them. Then, he expects Israel to treat the foreign people among them in the way he treated them.

The story of Israel had a slow start with the patriarchs (Abraham, Isaac, and Jacob and his sons) living as a vulnerable ethnic minority in Canaan. Their time spent as a small family of aliens was important for Israel's identity formation later in their story. Times are always challenging for outsiders, but the story became deeply threatening when famine drove Jacob's family to Egypt in the days of Joseph. In the empire of Egypt, their vulnerability increased dramatically.

The Hebrews showed up as economic refugees in Egypt and were initially welcomed because God had used the envy of Joseph's brothers to get Joseph to Egypt as a slave who turned into a Prime Minister, who ended up saving not only his family, but all of Egypt. Joseph forgave his brothers and gave his family privileged status in Egypt. But they were still foreigners with customs that were despised by Egyptians, and things turned against them when Joseph was out of the picture. God's blessings on Israel made them a nation of envy and suspicion by the Egyptians. When they grew large and the Egyptian "nationals" feared they were losing control of their culture and power, a new regime rose up and oppressed them.

The policy "Egypt for Egyptians" or "Egypt first" turned the empire toward exclusion and violence, and the Hebrews became a suffering people in great distress who could not save themselves. Even someone with the power and connections of Moses, who by God's grace ended up in the palace, could not save them. Their situation looked hopeless based on how power works in this world.

Before we go any further, we should read what God says to Moses when he appeared to him in the burning bush on Mount Sinai in Exodus 3:7-12 (NIV):

> The Lord said, "I have indeed seen the misery of my people in Egypt. I have heard them crying out because of their slave drivers, and I am concerned about their suffering. So I have come down to rescue them from the hand of the Egyptians and to bring them up out of that land into a good and spacious land, a land flowing with milk and honey—the home of the Canaanites, Hittites, Amorites, Perizzites, Hivites and Jebusites. And now the cry of the Israelites has reached me, and I have seen the way the Egyptians are oppressing them. So now, go. I am sending you to Pharaoh to bring my people the Israelites out of Egypt."
>
> But Moses said to God, "Who am I that I should go to Pharaoh and bring the Israelites out of Egypt?"
>
> And God said, "I will be with you. And this will be the sign to you that it is I who have sent you: When you have brought the people out of Egypt, you will worship God on this mountain."

It had been so long since Israel had heard from the God of Abraham, Isaac, and Jacob that they had essentially forgotten him because it seemed as if he had forgotten them. But that was far from the truth. God tells Moses that he had "seen their misery," had "heard their cries," cared about their suffering, and was "coming down" to rescue them.

God is not a distant creator who got bored with this creation and went on to other concerns. No, he is always aware and involved. This world is not just an experiment that interests him intellectually—he is emotionally invested. The Bible reveals a God who acts in the world to keep his promises, establish justice, protect his people, and complete his mission. He is a God of deliverance for the oppressed. He is a God who saves, not just in the afterlife, but in this life.

God sees, knows, and feels the mistreatment of oppressed people and acts accordingly out of his love for them. Israel started out in this story as refugees because of famine. At first, they were welcomed into the foreign land of Egypt. But regime change and fear of the size of this growing ethnic minority caused the Egyptians to worry they were losing control of their nation and culture, and they turned on the Hebrews and oppressed them with the genocidal policy of killing all the baby boys. Israel was stripped of their humanity and reduced to a trapped underclass without rights or hope in the world. God would not tolerate this. He acted to save and redeem.

This is not just a story about Israel; it is a paradigm of the God who acts in the world to liberate and bless people. Any people who claim to follow this God will share his ways—stay informed and be vigilant about the oppressive power of governments, industry, and even religious institutions. People who follow this God will intentionally commit to see and know what it's like for the oppressed, share their pain, and act for justice on their behalf. **If we allow our churches to be cultural sanctuaries for the privileged who do not see, touch, care for, or serve those on the margin, we are not following the model of the exodus or the cross.** Participating in God's salvation will always draw us into the same kind of service we see God demonstrating in his acts of salvation.

In Exodus 6:6-8 (NIV) God's salvation is described this way:

"Therefore, say to the Israelites: 'I am the Lord, and I will bring you out from under the yoke of the Egyptians. I will free you from being slaves to them, and I will redeem you with an outstretched arm and with mighty acts of judgment. I will take you as my own people, and I will be your God. Then you will know that I am the Lord your God, who brought you out from under the yoke of the Egyptians. And I will bring you to the land I swore with uplifted hand to give to Abraham, to Isaac and to Jacob. I will give it to you as a possession. I am the Lord.'"

Notice how comprehensive God's saving activity is. As Christopher Wright points out, Yahweh promises them four kinds of deliverance or freedom:

- Political—freedom from an oppressive regime that demanded total subservience.
- Economic—freedom from exploitation of labor (slavery) and inability to own land or the product of their labor.
- Social—freedom from being treated as an inhuman subclass or race.
- Spiritual—freedom from the obligation to worship the king and his state-supported gods.[15] (By the way, all the plagues are attacks on the gods of Egypt.)

Notice that God's salvation always starts with God's actions and operates on grace from first to last. Israel does nothing to cause God to save them. God acts based out of his compassion and because of his faithfulness to his promises to Abraham and the patriarchs. The Hebrew people benefit from the faithfulness and goodness of God without doing anything to distinguish themselves. However, once saved, they are called and sent to be God's instrument in the world, which is also a matter of God's grace. They are not better than others. **Election is not about superiority, but responsibility.**

Salvation is also comprehensive. It involves every phase of life: political, economic, social, and spiritual. No real salvation addresses only some of these aspects. **Churches who offer people freedom from their personal sins in a future heaven, but don't work to free people from the collective sins of society, or their oppressors, are not offering the same kind of salvation God does.** We cannot fulfill our mission and turn blind eyes toward evil done around us or be silent in the face of great injustice. On the other hand, if churches who work for political, economic, and social freedom for the vulnerable and oppressed don't also focus on turning them into worshippers of their redeeming God, they have lost a critical aspect of God's mission. God cares about and works for the total blessing and liberation of humans in

---

[15] Christopher J.H. Wright, *The Mission of God: Unlocking the Bible's Grand Narrative,* pp. 268-269.

every phase of life. This total well-being is what the Hebrew language means by peace or *shalom*. Every part of life should come under the reign of God when he is recognized as King.

God's salvation touches every part of people's lives, but it ultimately is not about humans. It is about God and his purpose. Here is how it is explained in Exodus 9:13-16 (NIV):

> Then the Lord said to Moses, "Get up early in the morning, confront Pharaoh and say to him, 'This is what the Lord, the God of the Hebrews, says: Let my people go, so that they may worship me, or this time I will send the full force of my plagues against you and against your officials and your people, so you may know that there is no one like me in all the earth. For by now I could have stretched out my hand and struck you and your people with a plague that would have wiped you off the earth. But I have raised you up for this very purpose, that I might show you my power and that my name might be proclaimed in all the earth.

God only allowed Egypt (Pharaoh) to become a world power so that he could use them to display God's power and character before all the world. As much as God cares about Israel and justice, God has a much larger purpose beyond rescuing the Hebrew people. He wants to be known by all nations. He has a global mission to set all things right again. That starts by making himself known to all.

There has always been a conflict between the God who rightfully reigns and all human attempts to reign, which are embodied in the world's kingdoms, republics, and empires. God used Joseph to build Egypt into an empire that he could then take down to display his power, glory, and mercy to the entire world. There is more at stake in this story than the liberation of Israel, as important as that is. This story is also about God revealing his power to raise up empires and bring them down because of his incomparable might. He has no rivals. But how does he use this power? Not to oppress the weak or use them mercilessly to serve himself, but to liberate them from those who abuse power to dehumanize others.

The scriptures make it clear that God does take sides in this world. He takes sides with the outsiders and oppressed, and he empowers the vulnerable. God is not completely impartial. He loves all people and all nations, but he opposes the proud and draws near to the humble. He takes sides against arrogant, bully nations and empires who always demand not only excessive loyalty but worship. When kings or empires begin to demand to be treated like gods and turn natural patriotism into a nationalistic religion, they have set themselves up as rivals with the true King and ruler of the earth, and he will take them down.

Once we understand that the gospel starts in the Old Testament with Abraham and understand salvation through the lens of the first salvation story in the Bible (the exodus), Jesus' and the apostles' gospel will become much more comprehensible and comprehensive. Our failure to appreciate the OT background for the gospel has caused many in the modern west to reduce salvation to mere personal "sin management" so each of us can enter the afterlife as individuals.[16] That just won't do if you have a deeper understanding of salvation rooted in the whole counsel of God.

Once we see this aspect of the gospel, it is easier to understand how American slaves could take on the religion of their oppressive slave masters. Though they were denied access to literacy, in the balconies of their master's churches, they heard the biblical stories. Because of their social location, they heard a deeper story which their masters missed. They heard of a God who cared about slaves and was on their side. Of course, this story captured the attention of the American slaves and their descendants struggling for civil rights. The real mystery is how it was possible for White slave owners to read the OT and still support slavery and oppression.[17]

The slaves in the U.S. and people of color in Jim Crow America were drawn to this story, which is reflected in the spirituals they sang and the role the Black church played in the struggle for civil rights. This is still true of many of their heirs who face ongoing racial injustice, though some have been repelled by the legacy of a slaveholder religion. Many people have been attracted to the God who liberates the oppressed people of every nation, whether in North Korea,

---

[16] Cf. Dallas Willard, *The Divine Conspiracy: Rediscovering Our Hidden Life in God*, pp. 35-59.
[17] For a thoughtful treatment of the question, see Howard Thurman, *Jesus and the Disinherited*.

victims of human trafficking in Southeast Asia, or refugees fleeing Islamic extremism today. Salvation rightly understood is not just an otherworldly affair. People need saving in many ways.

The full implication of this story is hard to hear for people of any powerful nation that dominates its neighbor from the west or the east. It is certainly difficult for Christians of European descent in the world's superpower nations, like the U.S. We feel torn between our love for our country and abhorrence at how our nation has sometimes used its power in the world. In our patriotism, we quickly forget about how we held captive Japanese Americans during WWII or performed medical experiments on Puerto Ricans. [18] We would never have permitted this to be done to "White" Americans on the mainland. America is not uniquely prone to abuse its power. This is a human tendency that is part of every history of every culture. However, neither is the USA uniquely innocent. We have a lot to account for as a nation and we cannot avoid our responsibility by saying, "We aren't the only nation with atrocities in our history."[19]

Our temptation is to minimize our own nation's abusive use of power or to reject our nation completely. The challenge is to hold on to both our appropriate love for our homeland and people and also our Kingdom values that call on us to love and welcome all people, face hard truth, repent of our silence, and find ways to speak up for justice in Jesus' name.

This story still challenges God's people to capture a fully-formed sense of salvation God wants to bring to people (political, economic, social, and spiritual). We need to be asking questions like:

- How do we avoid reducing salvation to only an afterlife-oriented message?
- How can we respond in a God-like way to racial injustice, human trafficking, systemic oppression, refugees, and oppressive powers in our world today?

---

[18] For more about such events, read *How to Hide an Empire,* by Daniel Imerwahr.
[19] Cf. Richard T. Hughes, *Myths America Lives By: White Supremacy and the Stories that Give Us Meaning.*

Salvation and calling go together—they are one and the same. When God saves people, he calls them to give him glory and treat others the way he treated us. Saved people should remember that we were once refugees, vulnerable immigrants, and people without hope, in slavery of many kinds, when God saved us. Almost all Americans are immigrants to this country, even though it may be a century or more since our families arrived on this continent. Like Israel, it is healthy for us to remember how we came to be here. If we do, we can welcome others in similar situations and treat them as God treated us to his glory and for their blessing. This is how we extend the mission to be a blessing to all nations.

None of us can address every type of evil in the world, but we can all choose to engage injustice somewhere. We should all pray that God will show us how and where to advocate for people who are trapped in some oppressive sin-driven slavery either in our city or somewhere in the world, and investigate ways to be a force for love, justice, and freedom for them. We can't rescue all oppressed people everywhere. But we can speak up for and stand with those who are being mistreated near us.

We can also do things like going out of our way to eat and shop in a part of town where we are minorities. We can start conversations with people we meet and get to know them just to understand what their lives are like. We can seek to learn and appreciate the strengths of their culture. We can learn from them what their people need and work with them to help them with their dreams. We can do like God and go see, listen, care, and take appropriate action to help the oppressed locally and globally.

Putting this into practice

1. Educate yourself about the history of race and imperialism/colonialism and how it continues to impact our world.
2. Reach out to leaders of churches in your area that serve ethnic minorities. Ask them about their history, their vision, and ask how you can help them with what God is calling them to do.
3. Go out of your way to eat and shop in a part of town where you are a minority. Reflect and journal on how that felt. Try doing this at

least once a month. Start conversations with people you meet and get to know them just to understand what their lives are like.

4. Pray that God will call you to some people/group who are trapped in some oppressive sin-driven slavery either in this city or somewhere in the world, and investigate ways to be a force for love, justice, and freedom for them. Identify community leaders among those people and listen to them. Follow their lead.

Chapter 8:

Israel: One for All and All for One
Why We Can't Just Skip Most of the OT and Talk about Jesus

Imagine a teenager had the following conversation with her grandfather:

> "Grandpa, I really don't think I understand our family. I want to know who we are and where we come from. Can you tell me the story of our family?"

> "Sure. Well, right after I got here from the terrors of war and poverty in the old country, I met your Granny at a dance, and I was struck down with love at first sight. But when I asked her to dance, she turned me down, and I went home broken-hearted, determined I was going to win her back. The next thing I know, you were born to your parents and that has been the greatest blessing of my life."

Would this be a good response to the teenager's question? Not likely. It is just missing too many pieces. The teenager wants to know more than how her grandparents met. She wants to know about their home country. Why the family left there and came here and all the big pieces of the family story since. Identity comes from the larger story. We find out who we are by seeing how "our people" have lived in thick narratives over time. Beginnings matter, but they are not all that matters.

Yet, too often, we skip so much when we tell the gospel that we lose the identity and character of God and his people in the stripped-down version. Some things can't be hurried. Abbreviations can be helpful, but they leave out important pieces that need to be filled in to understand anything deeply. No one's life was transformed by Cliff's

Notes. Overviews and outlines may help you pass a test, but they don't leave a lasting impact on us.

Yet too often in trying to explain Jesus, Christians jump from a surface overview of Genesis 1-3 (creation and fall) to Jesus' crucifixion and resurrection, without even talking about his life. Then we ask the people listening to make a decision to follow Jesus and be baptized without knowing what it would look like to follow him. We are offering a mere transaction to secure an afterlife, not offering a model for how to live this life. But that is all we can ask for with such a limited story. There is no way for people to live out the story of Jesus well if they don't have some understanding of Genesis 4 to Malachi 4, not to mention the Gospels. The entire work of God between the Garden of Eden and Golgotha is not irrelevant to salvation. Without understanding God's work with Israel, the Gospels will be confusing at best, Acts will have many odd features, and much of what Paul and the other writers in scripture say will be opaque.

We are so anxious to get to the part of the story that is immediately relevant to the seeker's eternal destiny that we don't really help them see the bigger story that includes the people of God through time, and their role in joining the people of God now. Then we wonder why people don't feel connected to the people of God and find the Bible confusing. That just doesn't make sense. The Bible doesn't work that way. Neither does spiritual formation. While not every gospel presentation can tell the whole story of God, they should all fit within that larger story and have clear hooks to draw people into that larger story. While Jesus is the centerpiece of God's work, and a good starting place, it is a mistake to leave out Israel if we want to understand and advance God's mission. It is even a bigger mistake to leave out the life of Jesus in our desire to explain the meaning of his death.

Much of the problem is that we have lost a sense of what God is up to in the world. If we think the goal is for God to snatch as many individual, disembodied souls up to an otherworldly spirit heaven after this world is demolished (or beyond the grave), then his work in Israel won't have much meaning. Israel becomes little more than an incubator for Jesus—a people whose sole purpose is to produce the Messiah. But why would God work with this people for a few thousand years before Jesus came? Why not just start with Jesus instead of Abraham?

The answer is that God was seeking something we tend to overlook. God's end game is to restore the entire creation and rule over it as King. He even invites the creatures he made in his image to share in this reign with him (cf. 2 Timothy 2:12). Before he sought to reestablish his reign over all places and people, he started with one particular place and people. Israel is the prototype people of God and Palestine is the prototype land of God's people in a larger mission that will eventually encompass all places and people in all of creation.

Israel is like the concept car that designers produce before the factory starts mass production. Israel is like a model home in what is to be a huge neighborhood. Israel, especially as it is conceived and described in the Law of Moses and the Prophets, is a model of what a nation (people and land) that belongs to God entirely should be like. It was intended to be a showroom, a prototype, a living display of love, justice, grace, and holiness that the entire world could look at and say, "That's the life we want" and come streaming into Jerusalem (e.g., Psalm 86:9; Isaiah 25:6-8; Isaiah 60:1-9).

This is illustrated well in the exodus story. When God rescued Israel, it wasn't just about keeping his promises to the patriarchs (Abraham, Isaac, and Jacob) or even rescuing an oppressed people. It was always about his mission that extends to us today: to redeem, reconcile, and restore all nations in peace. After the exodus and defeat of Pharaoh's army at the Red Sea, God brings Israel to Mount Sinai and explains what he has done, why he has done it, and gives them instructions about what it means to live in this world as his chosen people. This is summarized in the Ten Commandments in chapter 20 and the rest of the Law of Moses (The Book of the Covenant). But he sets these instructions in an important larger context that explains Israel's mission in the world. If we don't understand this, we will misunderstand the Ten Commandments and all the instructions that follow about how to be a holy people.

Before both accounts of the Ten Commandments, God explains the purpose of Israel's salvation and how it relates to their mission in the world. It should be illegal to read the Ten Commandments in Exodus 20 without at least reading Exodus 19. Along with lots of instructions about not touching the mountain while he is speaking to the people, God tells Moses the following in Exodus 19:1-6 (NIV):

On the first day of the third month after the Israelites left Egypt—on that very day—they came to the Desert of Sinai. After they set out from Rephidim, they entered the Desert of Sinai, and Israel camped there in the desert in front of the mountain.

Then Moses went up to God, and the Lord called to him from the mountain and said, "This is what you are to say to the descendants of Jacob and what you are to tell the people of Israel: 'You yourselves have seen what I did to Egypt, and how I carried you on eagles' wings and brought you to myself. Now if you obey me fully and keep my covenant, then out of all nations you will be my treasured possession. Although the whole earth is mine, you will be for me a kingdom of priests and a holy nation.' These are the words you are to speak to the Israelites."

This is the call of Israel to live out what God promised Abraham from the beginning. Israel was not called for her own sake, but to serve as God's intermediary to all nations. This is a priestly calling that was given to the nation as a whole. Israel did nothing to deserve their salvation from Egypt. They did not save themselves in any way and the law which follows is not a list of what they must do to be saved. It is a description of how, as a saved people, they should embody God's calling to reveal him to all nations. God did not save Israel for Israel's sake but for the sake of all nations. They are a priest nation among all the nations—an intermediary. Israel's election as God's special people is not an honor that makes them better than the other nations, it is a responsibility to be God's instrument to reach all nations.

This is what priests do; they foster a relationship between God and people. They represent people to God, and they represent God to people. That is why they are to be holy, because they represent a holy God and are to be God's instrument to other nations. (See Deuteronomy 4:1-8).

Israel's performance was up and down through the years. At times they honored God, made him known to the nations, and drew people to him from other peoples. But often they didn't. Too often they copied the evil ways and false gods of other nations, lost their distinctiveness, and did not fulfill their mission.

King David, the prototypical king in many ways, finally led Israel to possess all the land God promised to them and established a nation exclusively devoted to the Lord. Despite his personal weaknesses and glaring failures, David tolerated no idols and trusted in the Lord alone. Under his reign, God led Israel to a time of unprecedented freedom and blessing, which extended through the golden era of Solomon. However, David was never the one truly reigning as king. He was a living symbol of the true King of Israel, the Lord God Almighty, which he freely acknowledged (cf. 1 Samuel 8; 2 Samuel 7). Because of his exclusive loyalty to Yahweh, David became the model of a king to come who would do for the whole world what David did for Israel. That is, he established the unchallenged reign of God over his people, put down all enemies, and established peace and well-being (*shalom*) for all the nations—Jesus is a real King with a real realm (the whole earth).

But, ultimately, Israel failed to fulfill their mission. They lost their distinctiveness and rejected God's purpose for their nation. So, God allowed them to be overrun and defeated for a while, even to be carried away into captivity, to learn from their mistakes and purify them. But God rescued them from Babylonian captivity in a second Exodus, enabled them to rebuild Jerusalem and the temple, and called them back to his original purpose.

Isaiah says it this way in Isaiah 42:6-7, 49:1-7 (NIV)

"I, the Lord, have called you in righteousness;
    I will take hold of your hand.
I will keep you and will make you
        to be a covenant for the people
        and a light for the Gentiles,
    to open eyes that are blind,
        to free captives from prison
        and to release from the dungeon those who sit in darkness.

Listen to me, you islands;
    hear this, you distant nations:
Before I was born the Lord called me;

from my mother's womb he has spoken my name.
He made my mouth like a sharpened sword,
　　in the shadow of his hand he hid me;
he made me into a polished arrow
　　and concealed me in his quiver.
He said to me, "You are my servant,
　　Israel, in whom I will display my splendor."
But I said, "I have labored in vain;
　　I have spent my strength for nothing at all.
Yet what is due me is in the Lord's hand,
　　and my reward is with my God."
And now the Lord says—
　　he who formed me in the womb to be his servant
to bring Jacob back to him
　　and gather Israel to himself,
for I am honored in the eyes of the Lord
　　and my God has been my strength—
he says:
"It is too small a thing for you to be my servant
　　to restore the tribes of Jacob
　　and bring back those of Israel I have kept.
I will also make you a light for the Gentiles,
　　that my salvation may reach to the ends of the earth."
This is what the Lord says—
　　the Redeemer and Holy One of Israel—
to him who was despised and abhorred by the nation,
　　to the servant of rulers:
"Kings will see you and stand up,
　　princes will see and bow down,
because of the Lord, who is faithful,
　　the Holy One of Israel, who has chosen you."
(emphasis added)

Much later, we can see that God actually used the years of exile
to set up his mission to come through Jesus. The scattering of the Jews
in the exile spread the people of God and the word of God among all
the nations of the world, setting up the later rapid expansion of the
gospel among people who knew scripture and God's story.

These odd immigrants, with their cultural heritage centers and weekly scripture-reading meetings (synagogues), scattered among all nations, preserved and taught the Word of God around the world between the Babylonian exile and spread of the gospel. This meant that there was a nucleus of people almost everywhere who had some understanding of God, his story, character, and ways, who could serve as a foothold in every nation as the gospel was preached first in those places.

The early church started in the synagogues among the Jewish diaspora. Almost every church mentioned in the NT began out of a synagogue, and the early leaders of these churches were formed among people steeped in God's story. The early apostles and evangelists could refer back to the stories of God, the promises and prophets, to show that God had been preparing for Jesus for thousands of years. In every way, Israel prepared the way for the gospel/kingdom to go global.

Israel is a constant reminder that the gospel is not just about harvesting individual souls but about forming a people suitable to inhabit and extend God's reign over a redeemed world. Israel, a nation, is an essential reminder that God is seeking to form a people, not just rescue individuals. God is intent on creating the New Israel (represented by the New Jerusalem in Revelation 21-22) which is comprised of all nations (cf. Romans 9-11, esp. 11:11-32). The church is its own underground nation, whose borders will one day be all of a restored creation. The church is called to be a distinct people in the world who submit to God's reign, extend that reign as his agents, and live under his blessing and protection as his beloved children, servants, and partners in his global mission to redeem and restore all places.

The implications of this epic story are staggering. God is not just interested in our minds or our spirits, he is interested in all of us as individuals and communities and nations. He didn't ask us merely to understand him or agree with him, but to submit to him, reflect his character, and reign over the earth with him in peace and love. This objective requires we live out our life in Christ together as a distinct people in the world. But our obedience doesn't earn us God's love or salvation—it reflects his character, gives him glory in the world, and draws people who are tired of the lies and evil in the world to a better option. That isn't something we can do alone; it requires we be a different kind of people. The church doesn't exist primarily for our sake, but for the sake of those who don't know Jesus and haven't learned of the love and life of God available to them.

You can't be a Christian by yourself. It takes a community. That is more than attending events in a building (as we all learned during the COVID-19 pandemic); it is about a communal life together that models a different way of being. We are to display God's love, justice, mercy, and salvation. **The gospel is only as credible as the people who claim to believe it in any community.** Holiness, mercy, and service are essential for us to correctly reveal God to the world and accomplish his mission. But, ultimately, we can just point to the one who saved us, calls us, and give people previews of the end.

Putting this into practice

Reflecting on Israel and their role in the mission of God should lead us to ask the following questions:
1. Who is our kingdom community? Are we really a community or just a people who attend common events?
2. How do we live out community?
3. Who sees our community? How does it "shine its light" instead of "hide under a bushel?" What is the public aspect of our kingdom community and how does it model something unique that the world longs for?
4. How can our community group make God look beautiful and create an attraction to him for the people in your world?
5. Resign your small groups and larger church practice to more authentic community that models an alternative life to your city.

Chapter 9:

God Among the Nations: Every Knee Shall Bow
Why All Those Annoying Oracles to Foreign Nations?

What is the most Godforsaken place you've ever been? While it is understandable if your mind jumps to some desolate place where even cactus struggles to grow, that isn't what I mean. I'm talking about a place where you felt a presence so dark that God seemed completely absent. Perhaps it was an urban slum where there seemed to be no hope and lots of violence, desperation, and anger. Perhaps it was after a natural disaster where everything was chaos, ruin, and suffering. Perhaps it was a seedy area of town where vices that trapped and used people with blatant lies were promoted and almost celebrated.

I can think of several such places. I remember being in a Southeast Asian mega-city which is the epicenter of human trafficking or in a slum in a middle eastern city surrounded by angry looking men who gave us cold stares as they sat surrounded by symbols of sympathy for radical Islam. I have wept while walking through cardboard slums packed with hundreds of thousands of people in underdeveloped cities of the world. There are some incredibly dark places in our world.

Yet is there any place so dark that there is no light at all? Is there any place in the world where God is completely absent? Are there places God has abandoned? According to Psalm 139:7-12 (NIV), the answer is no:

> Where can I go from your Spirit?
>   Where can I flee from your presence?
> If I go up to the heavens, you are there;
>   if I make my bed in the depths, you are there.
> If I rise on the wings of the dawn,
>   if I settle on the far side of the sea,
> even there your hand will guide me,
>   your right hand will hold me fast.
> If I say, "Surely the darkness will hide me

and the light become night around me,"
even the darkness will not be dark to you;
the night will shine like the day,
for darkness is as light to you.

Even in the worst places, God is still there, to some degree. There is no darkness so deep, that God is completely hidden or obliterated.

Now think about the best person you've ever known who wasn't a Christian. Have you known some noble-hearted people who were "close to the kingdom," as Jesus used to say? Most of us have known people who had many God-like qualities but who just could not or would not accept Jesus as Lord. I've known some non-believers in Jesus who could stack up on morality with some of the most mature believers, if we are only talking about moral uprightness or self-discipline. There was a strong residue of God's ways in those people even if they didn't recognize its source and would not give God glory for it.

Because God created everything and is everywhere, traces of his creativity and character remain everywhere we go, even if it is greatly muted. Because God created everyone, and because he made humans in his image, there is some spark of the divine in every person, and no inhabited place is completely bereft of his presence. That means there is no person and no place beyond his reach.

Paul attests to the omnipresence of God while he was in Lystra, a place that seemed very dark and ignorant of God, in Acts 14:11-17(NIV):

> When the crowd saw what Paul had done, they shouted in the Lycaonian language, "The gods have come down to us in human form!" Barnabas they called Zeus, and Paul they called Hermes because he was the chief speaker. The priest of Zeus, whose temple was just outside the city, brought bulls and wreaths to the city gates because he and the crowd wanted to offer sacrifices to them.
>
> But when the apostles Barnabas and Paul heard of this, they tore their clothes and rushed out into the crowd, shouting: "Friends, why are you doing this? We too are only

84

human, like you. We are bringing you good news, telling you to turn from these worthless things to the living God, who made the heavens and the earth and the sea and everything in them. In the past, he let all nations go their own way. Yet he has not left himself without testimony: He has shown kindness by giving you rain from heaven and crops in their seasons; he provides you with plenty of food and fills your hearts with joy."

This was not a place filled with the Spirit of God. It was a pagan backwater where the worship of idols and fear-based superstitions ruled the day. Yet, Paul says that God has left some testimony (or evidence) of his truth everywhere.

Just because God did not force people to honor him or follow his commands—i.e., God let most of the nations of the earth "go their own way" for a period of time—did not mean that he didn't care about them or had given up on them. This is clearly stated all over the Bible, but especially in the prophets like Isaiah and Micah.

In Isaiah 2:2-4 (NIV):

In the last days
the mountain of the Lord's temple will be established
    as the highest of the mountains;
it will be exalted above the hills,
    and all nations will stream to it.
Many peoples will come and say,
"Come, let us go up to the mountain of the Lord,
    to the temple of the God of Jacob.
He will teach us his ways,
    so that we may walk in his paths."
The law will go out from Zion,
    the word of the Lord from Jerusalem.
He will judge between the nations
    and will settle disputes for many peoples.
They will beat their swords into plowshares
    and their spears into pruning hooks.

Nation will not take up sword against nation,
nor will they train for war anymore.

In Micah 4:1-5 (NIV), we read:

In the last days
the mountain of the Lord's temple will be established
as the highest of the mountains;
it will be exalted above the hills,
and peoples will stream to it.
Many nations will come and say,
"Come, let us go up to the mountain of the Lord,
to the temple of the God of Jacob.
He will teach us his ways,
so that we may walk in his paths."
The law will go out from Zion,
the word of the Lord from Jerusalem.
He will judge between many peoples
and will settle disputes for strong nations far and wide.
They will beat their swords into plowshares
and their spears into pruning hooks.
Nation will not take up sword against nation,
nor will they train for war anymore.
Everyone will sit under their own vine
and under their own fig tree,
and no one will make them afraid,
for the Lord Almighty has spoken.
All the nations may walk
in the name of their gods,
but we will walk in the name of the Lord
our God for ever and ever.

Clearly, God was concerned with all nations, and not just Israel, long before sending Jesus. God had a strategy to reach all people groups before Jesus came. That was Israel. One constant theme through the OT was that all nations belonged to the one creator God who revealed himself to and through Israel. God's ultimate vision was to unite all the nations in a restored, just world through Israel.

One of Israel's big areas of confusion was what it meant to be God's chosen people. In scripture, election is not about privilege but responsibility. One of the common mistakes we see among Christians was also present among the Israelites throughout history, i.e., confusing calling (election) with superiority. This false sense of superiority quickly turns to judgmental exclusivity. Israel consistently gave in to the temptation, either to lose their distinctive identity and role by copying other nations, or to retreat into a smug superiority that distanced themselves in a condemning rejection of other cultures. Both responses are off mission and impede God's purpose for his people. God wants "every knee to bow" and "every tongue to confess" regardless of what color the knee or language of the tongue (cf., Philippians 2:9-11).

Israel was called to reach the nations, not escape the nations.[20] This is clearly stated throughout the OT, most notably among all the oracles for foreign nations in the prophetic books (cf. Amos 1-2). God called Israel to be his special nation in order to reach all nations. He never gave up on this calling and purpose. Israel and the nations will ultimately be saved together (cf. Romans 9-11). God always cared for, reached out to, worked among, and held accountable all the nations of the world. However, his special revelation was to and through Israel and later the church. God's missions for Israel to draw in all the nations became more overt for the church, which is comprised of people from every nation, and is God's instrument to unite all nations under his reign.[21]

Lest we deceive ourselves about the challenge of such a message, we should remember that when Jesus preached from Isaiah 61 about the Kingdom of God being for all nations (people groups) in

---

[20] This is true in general even though there were a few specific times and places where God used Israel as his instrument of justice on specific nations. The conquest of Canaan in particular is ethically complicated, to say the least. We cannot give it a full treatment within the scope of this book. This has been addressed in an earlier footnote but needs to be acknowledged here as well. While God did either tolerate or even command Israel to use violence toward specific nations at specific times, his ultimate aim was to unite the nations in a restored world.

[21] There is no similar call of the church to be God's instrument of judgement toward any nation at any time. Jesus rejected all violence and called his people to live in peace both praying for and loving our enemies. The early church rejected the use of all violence as incompatible with following Jesus and his teaching.

Luke 4, his hometown citizens ran him out of the synagogue and tried to kill him. Separating God's multi-national kingdom from the idolatry we build up around our countries, nation states, and empires has always been a challenge, but God is not willing to negotiate on this.

God's dream comes to complete fulfillment as the Bible ends in Revelation.

This is clear in the climactic end of the story in Revelation 21:22-22:5 (NIV):

> I did not see a temple in the city, because the Lord God Almighty and the Lamb are its temple. The city does not need the sun or the moon to shine on it, for the glory of God gives it light, and the Lamb is its lamp. The nations will walk by its light, and the kings of the earth will bring their splendor into it. On no day will its gates ever be shut, for there will be no night there. The glory and honor of the nations will be brought into it. Nothing impure will ever enter it, nor will anyone who does what is shameful or deceitful, but only those whose names are written in the Lamb's book of life.
>
> Then the angel showed me the river of the water of life, as clear as crystal, flowing from the throne of God and of the Lamb down the middle of the great street of the city. On each side of the river stood the tree of life, bearing twelve crops of fruit, yielding its fruit every month. And the leaves of the tree are for the healing of the nations. No longer will there be any curse. The throne of God and of the Lamb will be in the city, and his servants will serve him. They will see his face, and his name will be on their foreheads. There will be no more night. They will not need the light of a lamp or the light of the sun, for the Lord God will give them light. And they will reign for ever and ever.

Notice how many times God mentions "the nations" here. Just to clarify, as we saw in an earlier chapter, "nations" here does not mean "nation-states" in the modern sense. That kind of nation didn't exist yet. The kind of nation-states we think about today didn't develop until the last few centuries. The word here is *ethnos* (often translated "gentiles"), which refers to people groups with distinct languages and cultures (and usually but not always territory).

I find it fascinating that in this vision of the end of all things, the "nations" (people groups) are still present and celebrated. God wants to heal the nations with leaves from the tree of life, not obliterate all ethic distinctives. God is not just seeking to save individuals but nations. The New Jerusalem will be populated not just by people but by nations. When God's work is all done and everything restored, we will not be generic humans. We will we retain our national identities and cultures in some respect.

The cultural treasures of each nation will be carried into the celestial city of God by the leaders of the nations to be put on display in the eternal Kingdom of God. Why would God want these treasures present? Because they were made through the creative power of God which resides in all nations. That means they have lasting value. Even if people don't know where the creative power to make beauty comes from, God does, and he doesn't want all this artistic productivity to be lost.

It's hard to unpack all the implications of these insights, and we have to be careful about pressing apocalyptic imagery into overly literal interpretations. But it is clear that God does care about more than just saving disembodied, generic, individual souls. He plans to redeem and restore every culture, ethnic group, and people on the earth. God has left deposits of his image: his wisdom, goodness, and creativity, in all people groups, and he wants all of that saved for all time. God has been working among every people group in ways that we don't immediately see, and they don't realize, until they've come to know him fully.

We need to be looking for the evidence of God's work and wisdom among every people and use that as the bridge to build between people and Jesus. Just read Acts 18:7-11 (NIV):

> Then Paul left the synagogue and went next door to the house of Titius Justus, a worshiper of God. Crispus, the synagogue leader, and his entire household believed in the Lord; and many of the Corinthians who heard Paul believed and were baptized.

One night the Lord spoke to Paul in a vision: "Do not be afraid; keep on speaking, do not be silent. For I am with you, and no one is going to attack and harm you, because I have many people in this city." So Paul stayed in Corinth for a year and a half, teaching them the word of God.

The Apostle Paul was afraid to work in Corinth because it was such a notorious city filled with the evils typical of big port cities. Yet, God saw it differently. Unknown to Paul, God says he has people in this city. He clearly does not mean they are already disciples of Jesus. That is why Paul is there. What does he mean? I think he means that God had been working in the lives of noble-hearted truth seekers and preparing them for a deeper revelation and inclusion into his kingdom. God is always preparing people to encounter him and the Gospel. Again, that is what Paul says in Ephesians 2:10 (NIV):

> For we are God's handiwork, created in Christ Jesus to do good works, which God prepared in advance for us to do.

Or, recall John 4:34-38. The Samaritan woman at the well seemed like a God-forsaken person, but she was the person God had prepared to be the gatekeeper to her village. Jesus says the hardest work had been done before he and the disciples arrived to reap what God had been sowing in many ways.

Stories like this are common in scripture. There are lots of examples of seekers with some relationship to and knowledge of God outside of "God's holy nation" in scripture. For example, review the stories of Melchizedek (Genesis 14:18-20), Ruth (Book of Ruth), Balaam (Numbers 22-24), and Cornelius (Act 10).

God has some level of witness everywhere. By God's common grace among all people, the residue of being made in God's image, people groups everywhere have some evidence of God and some truth. Paul puts it this way in Romans 1:20 (NIV):

> For since the creation of the world God's invisible qualities— his eternal power and divine nature—have been clearly seen, being understood from what has been made, so that people are without excuse.

Every culture creates beauty and longs for the glory of the transcendent God who made them and seeks them. No people group gets everything wrong because God has left a deposit of his nature in everyone. Just because people don't have all the light they need, doesn't mean they are all evil and foolishness. God has not abandoned any people.

This is more than just an interesting idea. It is crucial to our mission. Following Jesus should make us humble and respectful of all people, and we should be looking for the good in them and use the good they do know to draw them to its source and fulfillment in Jesus. This is what Jesus commanded and the early believers modeled (though not without great difficulty and controversy).

The hard reality is, **we can't reach people we don't respect. We can't reach people we think God has abandoned and despises.** We can't reach people with God's love if we reject their culture as inherently evil and beyond redemption. We have to learn to love what is good about the people and cultures we are called to reach if we are going to see the beauty of these people's heritage be put on display in the eternal Kingdom. People don't have to abandon everything about their culture to come to Jesus. He will help them see what of their heritage came from God and is precious to him. We should not be promoting our ethnic heritage over others. Mission should not be about promoting the values of the western world. Granted, separating Christian from western values is a challenge at points, but it is worth serious reflection. We are all seeking to live out the values of the Kingdom of God. It is important that we look for the evidence of God's work among all nations and cultures, and long for this good to be displayed in the New Jerusalem.

For example, Christians in the USA tend to value work more than family. We don't admit it to ourselves, but we routinely leave family for a better job. We work more than we should to move up in our careers. We introduce ourselves by our occupations. Most cultures don't do that. Latino cultures in particular are built around family. They make time for family. Work is clearly secondary. They work hard, but work is built around family. When someone is sick and needs to go the doctor, lots of family go with them. Everything revolves around family. That is a God-like trait that can be a bridge to talking about Jesus and God's kingdom family.

Arab Muslims place very high priority on hospitality. Unlike Americans who would often rather meet in a restaurant and avoid having people in their homes, an Arabian family might delight in hosting people in their homes and will feed them until they burst. What a God-like quality! This is a bridge to talk about the kingdom of God where all are welcome.

Rwandan cultures, like many African people, love to dance. They express themselves through their bodies in beautiful ways. For someone who grew up in a culture that was uncomfortable with our bodies, and created dance-free zones, like me, this is surprising but also amazing. The church I grew up in taught that it was sinful to dance, probably because even God was offended when he saw us try. But when you see how some people from African cultures combine bodies and spirits to express joy, there is something divine on display that speaks of the resurrection body and the unity of humanity as body and spirit. That is a bridge to the kingdom of God.

I could go on to describe the singing of the South African peoples or gentleness of southeast Asian cultures. All people groups have cultural elements that reflect the glory of being created in God's image. William Easterly once wrote,

> Heaven is where chefs are French, police are British, lovers are Italian and car mechanics are German & it is all organized by Swiss. Hell is where chefs are British, police are German, lovers are Swiss, car mechanics are French and it is all organized by Italians.[22]

Every nation has art, music, stories, traditions, and endless cultural expressions and artifacts that need to be appreciated and drawn into the kingdom of God.

God loves all people and their cultures and is determined to draw a remnant from every people group into his kingdom so that no culture is lost forever. God is already working to reveal his love and call to everyone everywhere before anyone who knows him well arrives on the scene. People who are living out God's mission always step into existing stories everywhere we go and with everyone we meet.

---

[22] Williams Easterly, *The White Man's Burden, pp. 77-78.*

These core biblical insights may not be popular today in the USA, but they are still true. We don't like to hear it, but American exceptionalism is counter to the gospel. The idea that America is the new Israel and is a superior nation to all others is dangerously in error. We don't have to despise other nations or have a superiority complex to be patriotic, any more than we have to think all other families are inferior to love our family. Followers of Jesus are part of a nation called the Kingdom of God, which defines us far more than our country of origin. Just notice how clear this is in the following New Testament passages (all NIV):

Philippians 3:20

> But our citizenship is in heaven. And we eagerly await a Savior from there, the Lord Jesus Christ,

Hebrews 11:13-16

> All these people were still living by faith when they died. They did not receive the things promised; they only saw them and welcomed them from a distance, admitting that they were foreigners and strangers on earth. People who say such things show that they are looking for a country of their own. If they had been thinking of the country they had left, they would have had opportunity to return. Instead, they were longing for a better country—a heavenly one. Therefore God is not ashamed to be called their God, for he has prepared a city for them.

1 Peter 2:9-12

> But you are a chosen people, a royal priesthood, a holy nation, God's special possession, that you may declare the praises of him who called you out of darkness into his wonderful light. Once you were not a people, but now you are the people of God; once you had not received mercy, but now you have received mercy.

Dear friends, I urge you, as foreigners and exiles, to abstain from sinful desires, which wage war against your soul. Live such good lives among the pagans that, though they accuse you of doing wrong, they may see your good deeds and glorify God on the day he visits us.

Loving your country is a good thing for people from every nation. **Putting any country above the Kingdom of God or confusing our country with the Kingdom of God is dangerous and damaging to our witness and God's mission**. There is no telling the evil and suffering that has come from beliefs of national/racial superiority. Much of this has been done in the name of "civilizing and converting" the lost. Nothing obstructs the mission of God today as much as the legacy of colonialism and colonial abuses in missions.

The church is a nation without borders so all people can come in. There is no wall-building around this nation. The Kingdom of God is designed to be a multi-cultural display of the glory of God's work among all people groups for all eternity. God loves all the cultures of the world and wants to preserve all that is good in every people—all the evidence of his goodness and creative power. **The gospel does not obliterate our cultures or national identities; it purifies and amplifies all that is good about them.**

This is probably not going to be easily heard by "White" readers,[23] but we need to own and repent for our racial history and the residue of racist thoughts, feelings, and biases that are still embedded in our hearts and social structures (both in the church and larger society). We need to follow the examples of Daniel, Nehemiah, and Ezra and confess the sins of our ancestors and the ways we have perpetuated them consciously or unawares (chapter nine in all three books). This goes against the radical individualism of our culture but is very much in

---

[23] The concept of "Whiteness" as a united category of light skin toned people is historically new and biologically unjustified. It was created to justify the dominance of European people groups over other people groups. Who has been counted as "White" has shifted over the last four centuries. It is a propaganda myth that has no place in the Kingdom of God. For more on this subject see *Working Toward Whiteness: How America's Immigrants Became White: The Strange Journey from Ellis Island to the Suburbs* by David R Roediger. See also my blog entry "Why There Are No White People in the Bible" at https://www.mrnet.org/blog-db-1/2021/01/26cbh-s5y6g.

keeping with the scriptures and the gospel. This kind of repentance needs to be done communally, not just individually. Racism is a social matter that is embedded in all our social structures. Personal sorrow isn't enough. It needs to be exposed, owned, repented of, and changed. Remember what John the Baptist said to the Pharisees, "Bring forth fruit in keeping with repentance."

We don't have space to delve into this topic in much depth in this work and it is a subject worthy of many books. Fortunately, there are many good ones. I'll recommend some in a footnote here.[24]

Putting this into practice

1. Think about a culture, nation, or people group that you just don't like. We almost all have cultural biases against some cultures. Who do you have bias against that you encounter or who are moving into your city?
2. Commit to pray for these people and ask God to give you a heart for them. It would be good for you to do some simple research about them, their story, and look for evidence of their good qualities. Go out of your way to eat their food and interact among them with an eye to what is good about them.
3. Pray that God will open your eyes to the people around you that he is preparing to hear a word of hope from a believer in Jesus.
4. Try to start a conversation with people everywhere you go who seem foreign to you. Learn how to have conversations with people outside your normal social circles so you can learn how to have spiritual conversations with them.
5. When you hear about people and places around the world that seem particularly dark and evil, ask God to give you a love for them and feel his concern for them.

---

[24] *The Color of Compromise*, Jamar Tisby; *White Awake: An Honest Look at What It Means to Be White*, Daniel Hill; *Disunity in Christ: Uncovering the Hidden Forces that Keep Us Apart*, Christena Cleveland.

Chapter 10:

Big Salvation Story #2: The Cross
Why Can't God Just Say, "I Forgive You?"

I have an unhealthy habit I wish I could drop. I would be happier and have more peace if I could get this monkey off my back. But I just can't seem to stop myself. I'm a news addict. I never miss a day, often getting my fix multiple times a day. I'm not a hard-core news channel junkie. I don't watch MSNBC, CNN, or FOX News every evening, thank God. But I do watch a half hour of the evening news on a broadcast network, because I'm old. (If it tells you anything about how old, I really miss Peter Jennings.) I must also confess that I check news apps on my phone throughout the day and I follow news channels on Twitter. I have a problem.

Not only does this compulsive news checking distract me, it also discourages me and tempts me to live in constant outrage. The news is almost always sad and often heart-breaking. Most of the time there is nothing I can do about anything I learn except pray (which is nothing to dismiss). But do I need to know about all the world's troubles and outrages? Did God design us to carry that much trouble around with us? Probably not. It's more than any person can endure to know about so much pain.

So why do I do it? Because I want to know what is going on. Because I long to be part of a larger story in the world. Because my life makes more sense when I see how it fits within the events which shape the world. It's hard to know how to be me if I don't know what is happening around me. In the globalized world, "around me" is everywhere.

I think it is important that the various pieces that make up the news are called stories. They are supposed to be true stories (unlike much of the growth of fake news that we must contend with), but they are still "stories."[25] While news comes from different perspectives,

---

[25] Fake news is hardly a new thing. Every regime throughout time has done all they could to shape the narratives that were accepted by "their people."

which shape how it's told, ultimately news is not a form of philosophy or religion. It is a series of events. It is stories. Something has happened. What the stories mean for people depends on who they are, where they are, and how they see the world. But all people are responding to the same set of events—the same story.[26]

This impacts how we understand the significance of Jesus. Of all the ways the NT writers could have described the coming and work of Jesus in the world, they chose the word "gospel" which means "good news." The gospel is first and foremost news. Christianity is a story. Something happened. The Jesus event matters because it changed things. The world is different. We don't just think differently in the same world. We are in an altered world. It matters greatly that the early followers of Jesus called their message "gospel" or a "good news story" instead of a philosophy, law, code of conduct, or requirements for our own salvation. Our message is an event not an idea. God acted. Things are different now. It was one event (or collection of inter-related events) but it has many meanings depending on who you are, where you are, and how you see the world.

In Jesus' context of the Roman Empire, it had not been that long since Caesar Augustus had used the same Greek word translated "good news" to announce that he had become the new emperor. He conquered his enemy and put out the good news that his reign had commenced. At least it was good news for those who supported him. The good news about Jesus was similar news in this regard; it was announcing a new king had come to reign. But this king was going to be of a totally different type. Instead of killing his enemies, he would die for them and change the dynamics of the world forever. That was good news indeed for everyone who was oppressed by Rome, such as the Jewish people, and anyone who longed for a more just world or life with more meaning than the broken world we inhabit can provide.

No single event has the same meaning for all people. For example, if the government acts to cut taxes, that will help some people and hurt others. If the government decides to legalize marijuana, some people will rejoice, and others will be dismayed or outraged. It all depends on your values and interests. It depends on what story you

---

[26] For this entire way of thinking, I am deeply indebted to Mark Love who, at the time of this writing, teaches at Rochester College in Rochester, Michigan.

think you are in and what roles you play in those stories. If the government acts to reform immigration laws, some people will relax and feel safer. Others are put in grave danger and must watch their backs. One event has many meanings.

On 9-11, while most people throughout the USA were shocked and grieving, there was rejoicing in many Middle Eastern cities. There was only one event, but it had radically different meanings and produced diverse reactions from people who were living out of different stories and worldviews.

Likewise, the gospel is news. It is one multi-part event: the death, burial, and resurrection of Jesus.[27] For followers of Jesus, it is Good News. It is not the same old hopeless string of crimes, threats, disasters, tragedies, and atrocities we hear about every night. This is a story that offers to change the nature of all other news. But not everyone hears this news the same way and not everyone rejoices over it. It all depends on who you are, where you are, and how you see the world.

But, for most people, regardless of who they are, the gospel can be good news if they understand it properly. Most of the time, when people don't hear the story of Jesus as good news, it is because they have not heard it in a way that connects with them. They are not seeing the events of the gospel in a complete and beneficial way. They are hearing a reduction of the good news to ideas that may miss them or even threaten them.

One question that has bothered me for years is this: If the gospel is good news, why do we so often start gospel presentations with "You are condemned sinners?" Is that good news? Not really. It's hard to draw people toward you if you start a conversation by punching them in the face. That is not the offense of the gospel, it is something else. It may be true, but it isn't good news. The good news tells guilty people how God has made a way for them to be forgiven. The message is not one of guilt itself. Despite what many Christians seem to believe, the gospel is about much more than guilt management.

I know the prophets often confront their hearers with their sins pretty quickly. But, they were talking to insiders. They spoke to people

---

[27]Paul mentions a three-part event here. But the Gospels and Acts include life, death, burial, resurrection, and ascension. All are part of the Christ event which comprises the Gospel.

within a covenant that started with God's grace. Their hearers already knew the good news of God's actions on their behalf in history (e.g., The Exodus). For people who do not know God nor what he has done for them, the good news should probably start with, well, good news.

I fear that the way Christians in America talk about the gospel is very limited. It typically only sounds like good news to people who already feel guilty or feel like failures because of their own mistakes. It focuses on individual sins and personal guilt and offers people forgiveness and hope for salvation beyond this life. As true as this message is, does everyone you know in the world feel like a failure who is responsible for their own condition because of their mistakes? Hardly. If the only way we know to speak good news is to address people who feel like guilty failures, we are going to miss a lot of people, especially if they come from cultures not based on a guilt-innocence worldview.[28]

If the only way we know how to speak gospel is to offer relief for guilt, then we have to generate awareness of guilt. If people don't already feel guilty, we have to try to convince people they are guilty failures before we can share our word of hope. That doesn't sound like good news. Or, we can wait for them to crash and burn and then follow up with hope. But are those our only options? Is the gospel only a word of hope to people who see themselves as guilty failures? No, the gospel is good news to people who have experienced the brokenness of the world in every imaginable way.

In the NT it is clear that the gospel is bigger than having our guilt removed or forgiveness. The Bible uses many pictures of salvation and most don't address individual guilt. Yet, when Americans speak of the gospel, we almost exclusively use legal language from a courtroom. We talk about law-breaking, guilt, judgment, justice, justification, condemnation, and acquittal. For people who feel guilty or think in legal categories and know they have broken God's laws, this is good news.

But that is not how most people through time have naturally experienced the impact of sin in the world. This is one of the reasons that most of the time the Bible has a broader vocabulary than the American church. Scripture uses many images when discussing

---

[28] Cf. Jason George's *3-D Gospel.*

salvation or the gospel, and it speaks to a much broader audience. While the cross of Christ certainly addresses the problem of guilt, it also offers hope and salvation for every other way sin has damaged God's world, including shame, fear, powerlessness, emptiness, hopelessness, oppression, injustice, and death, to mention a few. To limit the gospel to a solution for guilt greatly reduces its ability to offer hope and restoration to the many people in all the world's cultures.

We need to broaden our understanding of the gospel to the full range of meanings found in our Bibles. Let's take a look at how the gospel sounds in different NT scriptures. As you read these scriptures, ask yourself how Jesus and the apostles present the Good News and how this differs from a message mainly focused on forgiveness for guilt. What is the problem in view and how is the gospel functioning as good news in each passage?

Mark 1:14 -15 (NIV)

After John was put in prison, Jesus went into Galilee, proclaiming the good news of God. "The time has come," he said. "The kingdom of God has come near. Repent and believe the good news!"

In this context, Jesus shows up in an occupied and oppressed nation and announces the long-awaited and promised Kingdom of God has finally arrived. This is a deeply communal and political message, even if it doesn't mean what people will assume it does on first hearing. It is political, not in the modern partisan sense of the world, because it has to do with a community of people and their rightful government under their true king. That changes their relationship with all other claims on their loyalty.

Mark 10:42-45 (NIV)

Jesus called them together and said, "You know that those who are regarded as rulers of the Gentiles lord it over them, and their high officials exercise authority over them. Not so with you. Instead, whoever wants to become great among you must be your servant, and whoever wants to be first must be slave of all.

For even the Son of Man did not come to be served, but to serve, and to give his life as a ransom for many."

In this context, Jesus is contrasting the nature of his reign with other rulers and other empires. The good news is that the coming Kingdom of God is not going to be oppressive, top-down control. Rather, this king will be a servant. He will not ask his people to sacrifice their lives for him, but he will die to ransom their lives from slavery. He will pay the price for their freedom. He will be breaking the shame-inducing powerlessness that people feel when some oppressive ruler has a boot on their necks. Jesus will victoriously confront the powers of this world (and spiritual powers who are behind them). Jesus will break that power through great personal sacrifice and establish a new use of power and honor in the world.

John 3:16 (NIV)

For God so loved the world that he gave his one and only Son, that whoever believes in him shall not perish but have eternal life.

In this context, salvation is pictured as eternal life. This involves more than just a life that goes on forever. The problem isn't just that we are going to die, but that all of life has the burnt taste of death in it here. The gospel is an offer for life of a different quality starting now. It is light, not darkness. It is being born again or born from above, as he tells Nicodemus earlier in this chapter. It is having life that comes from Spirit and not just flesh. It is life of a different quality altogether in a world where everything grows weak, old, and dies. It is having light (a life that makes sense) in a world of darkness (life that makes no sense).

2 Cor 5:17-19 (NIV)

Therefore, if anyone is in Christ, the new creation has come: The old has gone, the new is here! All this is from God, who reconciled us to himself through Christ and gave us the ministry of reconciliation: that God was reconciling the world to himself

102

in Christ, not counting people's sins against them. And he has committed to us the message of reconciliation.

Here salvation is described in relational or familial terms. It is a reconciliation between people whose relationship was broken by some offensive behavior that violated the relationship. The problem is not presented as broken laws but broken relationships. Jesus' solution is such a revolutionary action with such global consequences that it can only be described as a new creation. This is not a simple one-on-one relationship repair; it is a repair of all the relationships between God and his entire world. But it is relational, not legal, in nature. The offenses are not so much violations of law as violations of trust. The focus is not on the change of legal status but the repair of a lost relationship.

Col 2:15 (NIV)

"And having disarmed the powers and authorities, he made a public spectacle of them, triumphing over them by the cross."

Here, Paul uses the image of military victory over the evil powers that oppress people spiritually. It is a mixed metaphor in the larger context, but it is important to the image of the victorious King (Messiah) who has defeated the spiritual powers that hold people in terror and disarmed them and humiliated them in public by his death and resurrection.

What I hope you can see is that the gospel is good news in more ways than just offering removal of guilt. To borrow language from the movie *Titanic*, it saves us in every way a person can be saved.

Remember, the gospel is a story. It is an event. God acted. How that impacts you depends on who and where you are. To preach the gospel is to announce a world-transforming event where God entered history and acted decisively to change the world. The implications of that event strike different people somewhat differently depending on how they have felt the impact of the brokenness of the world.

This is critically important to understand if we are working with people who come from cultures that are more focused on honor-shame or power-fear instead of guilt-justification. Most cultures in the world are not guilt-based cultures. They have not experienced "the introspective conscience of the west."[29] They are shame-based or fear-based cultures. These cultures don't think of what is wrong with the world in terms of individual breaking of rules. Even in the post-Christian western world, guilt is fading as a concept and we are becoming much more oriented around shame and powerlessness. This is only accelerating with immigration and globalism.

For those who recognize and feel their guilt, the gospel certainly does offer a word of justification (i.e., forgiveness). For those who feel defective and untouchable (i.e., shame), it is a word of purification and beautification. For those who feel abandoned and alienated, it is a word of welcome, acceptance, and inclusion. For those who feel overwhelmed by the relentless power of evil in the world, it is a word of triumph over the principalities and powers that oppress "our people." For those who are trapped in a fear of death, it is a word of eternal life. For those who feel life is a pointless and empty void, it is a word of ultimate purpose and everlasting meaning.

Regardless of the way people experience the brokenness of the world, the cross speaks a word of hope and offers a new, bold logic for living differently in the world. This is the way of the cross and resurrection. It is the climax of God's work that fixes everything that is broken in our world. It is a model of life with an internal logic that should shape how we interact with the world. In order for us to fully utilize the power of the cross for mission, we need to understand the many ways it speaks hope and offers power for transformation in diverse cultures.

The cross is a multifaceted event with layers and layers of meaning. The death of Jesus was not just a legal gambit that gets us off the hook in a court of law; it is a complex event that shows us the character of God (his love and justice) and reveals the logic of how God's power works in the world.

The cross is not a vending machine where you put something in and get something out. It's not a magic formula. There is no "theory of the atonement" in the New Testament. That is, while every NT author references the cross in some way, there is no unified explanation for

---

[29] See Krister Stendahl, "The Apostle Paul and the Introspective Conscience of the West," in *Paul Among Jews and Gentiles.*

how the cross works to save us. Instead, there are a host of images with many different meanings (e.g., redemption, reconciliation, washing, justification, triumph, and on and on).

In the majority White North American context, shaped by the litigious culture of Western Europe, we have tended to overemphasize how the cross removes our legal guilt through justification. And we have focused on how it does this on an individual basis. But the gospel is much bigger than this, and our understanding of the gospel just doesn't resonate well with many cultures, including younger people from our own culture. We need a bigger and more robust understanding of the crucifixion and resurrection to live out our mission to the diversity of people we are sent to reach in our city and our world.

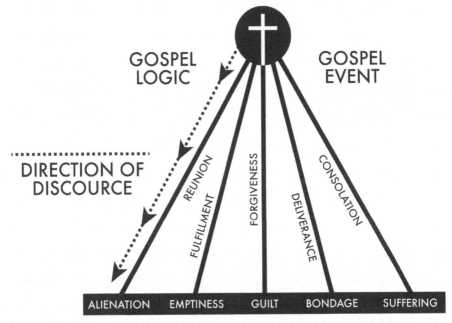

30

---

[30]The chart is based on concepts from W. Paul Jones' book *Theological Worlds.*

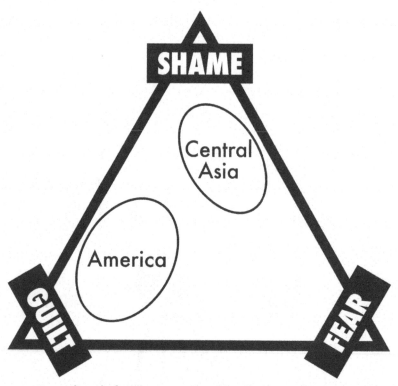

SHAME

GUILT

FEAR

Central Asia

America

Example only for illustration, not based on actual research.   31

I saw something once in an urban slum in Africa that stunned me. There was a young lady with no place to use the restroom. So, she urinated on the street. That happens in the U.S. also. But when this young lady did this, she pulled her skirt up over her head to hide her face. She was not afraid of breaking a rule (guilt), she was afraid of being shamed. She would rather expose her behind than her face. She was literally trying to save face. That is a very different way of thinking than what I had been raised to do. It was a reminder that people don't see the world the same way everywhere.

One common problem in many parts of the world is good church members who keep going to local shamans for healing when someone in their family is put under a curse or their children get sick. Western missionaries and national leaders who have been trained by

---

31 This chart comes from *The 3-D Gospel: Ministry in Guilt, Shame, and Fear Cultures* by Jayson Georges.

them are often perplexed about what to do. But if you understand the broader gospel dimensions it makes sense. These people have come to Jesus to have their sins forgiven so they can have a good afterlife. But the gospel they heard has offered them nothing to deal with the powers of the spiritual realm that terrorize them. They don't just need to know about forgiveness, they need to know about victorious Christ who defeated all the powers of evil. If our gospel doesn't deal with principalities and powers of this dark world, it will make weak converts and leave them wide open to the witch doctors.

This larger understanding of the gospel used to be more important for missions in other countries than in the U.S. We could assume most people understood the language of condemnation and forgiveness in America. It might not be their primary way of experiencing lostness, but they got it. They believed in a clear right and wrong and knew they were guilty of wrong. That is no longer a reliable assumption in the post-modern west.

In the U.S., we now live in a time when a diminishing percentage of people see themselves as guilty sinners who fear condemnation in eternal hell. But that doesn't mean they don't feel the impact of their brokenness. But to preach good news to all the nations (and all kinds of people here at home), we need to understand the broader message of the gospel.

We need to be able to explain how Jesus offers good news to people who experience sin as alienation or abandonment. Those who have been left behind, rejected, or abandoned don't need to be told their hurts are their fault. It's neither true nor kind. They need to hear a message about God's pursuit of them. They need a message of reconciliation and welcome into God's family.

For those who find life empty or meaninglessness, who feel like cosmic accidents in a mechanical universe devoid of purpose, we need to invite them to be part of God's mission to redeem and restore all creation. They need to know that behind the empirical world, is a transcendent being who gives their life enduring significance.

For those who have experienced bondage or oppression to spiritual powers, addictions, or social/political forces, they need to know that history is not written by the winners. History is written by the one who joined the suffering, accepted injustice and even death only to rise in triumph beyond the grave. We need to show them the

Jesus who is more powerful than all the forces of darkness and evil in the spiritual or earthly realms and defeated them in his death and resurrection.

For those trapped in suffering and decline unto death, we need to introduce them to a Jesus who has experienced our suffering and death and overcome it, giving it new meaning. They need a God who is not absent in suffering—he is doing powerful work even when we can't fully understand it.

The importance of the fuller gospel is hard to over-emphasize. For example, one of the greatest problems in the church is our racial failures. There are many reasons why people tend to gather into churches filled with people like themselves, but some of those reasons are theological. We won't overcome the barriers among churches without a gospel big enough to draw us all into one overarching story with the same God as the center.

One reason that churches in the U.S. tend to be racially segregated is that we don't feel the brokenness in the world in the same way. The majority White culture tends to view the world through individualistic lenses and focus on personal responsibility and guilt. They are seeking forgiveness. White culture has been in the power position and has accepted the individualism that works well in free market capitalist societies. White churches have focused on the gospel for individuals but have been less interested in focusing on systemic issues of justice and power, which is convenient for people in positions of prominence. God comes across as mostly concerned about personal righteousness (piety, morality).

But, for ethnic minorities, this is hardly adequate. People of color have lived for many generations with systemic injustice and oppression. From cradle to grave, everything is harder for people of color going back over 400 years. For this reason, churches of color tend to focus more on the issues of justice, honor, and power. They are looking for a God who will recognize their value, overthrow the forces set against them, and promise them deliverance from those who hold them down. They are looking for hope, empowerment, and justice as a people, not just as individuals.

Preaching about personal guilt and forgiveness has some value for people with this life experience but is not adequate in their lives. It can come across as victim blaming, which they have had to endure long enough. Churches of color see and celebrate aspects of the gospel that White churches often miss altogether. The same gospel speaks to both, but we only hear it well in the channel to which we are tuned. We are bewildered that others can't hear it as we do.

We live in a world that struggles to trust God because we expect life to make sense to us and it just doesn't. We are arrogant in the developed western world and demand God defend himself and his actions. While that attitude is not healthy, God does not shrink from the challenge and the gospel gives a powerful answer.

The cross shows us a God who can be trusted in a world of pain and injustice. The world recoils at the evil we see in this world and challenges God to justify allowing it to be so. People challenge either God's justice, power, love or all three. How can an all-powerful God care about us, care about justice, and have the power to fix the world and still allow this world to go on as it is?

While the Bible often reminds us that we are on dangerous ground when we try to drag God into court and make him defend himself (cf. The Book of Job and Romans 9), it also tells us of a God who answers these questions in a compelling way. God does not stand apart from a sinful and suffering world in judgment and just say, "Okay, I forgive you." That would trivialize the evil in the world and would lead many people to respond with, "Yes, but we can't forgive you back." Instead of just forgiving us and saying, "Why can't we just get along?" God treats the evil in the world as a serious problem that he can't just sweep away with an easy forgiveness.

Instead, God entered this broken world personally, experienced all the evil and suffering the world can offer us, and rose in triumph over it to show that his power to redeem is greater than the power of evil to destroy. God removes the sin of the world by absorbing it— taking it all on himself. Therefore, we can't accuse him of trivializing sin. He experienced injustice himself. And God raises up the son we killed, defeating all the powers of sin, shame, injustice, hopelessness, and death. God defends his good name and demonstrates his love of the world and justice in one bold move that creates a new reality available for all of us (cf. Romans 3).

I keep coming back to this point because it is important and often missed: The Gospel is a STORY. It connects with everyone differently, but it connects with everyone because it speaks to every kind of wrong, hurt, failure, and brokenness there is. We think about our lives in terms of stories, not abstract concepts. When we hear other people's stories, we listen in light of our story. When we hear a story with points of connection, we automatically want to tell our story or someone else's story back. People only change their lives when they hear or see a story that expands their vision of what their lives could become.

People who are estranged from God need to hear how their story can become part of God's story. We have to start with a word of hope for the hurts that people experience and feel. In a world of bad news, people need good news—a word of love, hope and care.

It is important that we know how the death, burial, and resurrection of Jesus is good news for us. But, if we want to be effectively on mission for God, we also need to know how it is good news for people who are not like us.

Putting this into practice

Here are some questions to explore with people as you are getting to know them to help you know how to speak Good News to them:
1. How have they experienced the bad news of sin in the world?
2. What kind of force or power are they working against?
3. What do they fear?
4. What are they seeking to conquer or overcome?
5. What kind of deliverance are they seeking?
6. Where does the Gospel story make "good news" contact with their story?
7. How can God's story reframe and redefine their stories?
8. How would you tell the Gospel story to these people?

Chapter 11:

The Church: Never-Ending Story of Jesus
Recovering the Life of Jesus

When you hear the word "church," what do you feel? How does it impact you emotionally? Is it a warm feeling of safety and security, like images of home? Is it an exciting feeling like preparing for a trip or new challenge? Or, is it an anxious, painful, or conflicted feeling?

What images come to your mind when you hear the word church? Do you see a building? Do you picture an event, such as corporate worship? What videos play in your head? What do those images trigger in your body? Where do you feel them? How do you explain the origin of these images and feelings?

Give yourself a few minutes with your eyes closed and picture the images that are produced by the word "church" and then monitor how your body and emotions are impacted. I know this is odd, but it will likely reveal things to you which you don't normally process at a conscious level, but which impact you just the same.

Now think beyond yourself. Is the word "church" a positive or negative word in our culture? Obviously, that is a complex question with many answers depending on who you are talking to and what their experience is. But what do you think is the dominant view of church in the larger culture? We routinely hear that Christians are often seen in America as judgmental, hypocritical, racist, anti-gay, anti-abortion, anti-everyone who is not like us.[32] This reputation is making Christian witness more and more difficult. Instead of the church taking the confession of sinners, the church should be making a confession of sin to the world. Until we repent and confess the historic sins of "our people," like Daniel, Ezra, and Nehemiah (all in the 9th chapter of their books, as it turns out), we will struggle to have credibility to those who

---

[32] For documentation of this, see the numerous books by Gabe Lyons and David Kinneman starting with *UnChristian*. For problems with racism, see Jamar Tisby, *The Color of Compromise*.

have been on the receiving end of the church's complicity with power and oppression in our culture.

One way to assess what you really think and feel about church is to reflect on how comfortable you are talking about Christian faith or your church in public. Do you fear to bring these matters up because you anticipate rejection or criticism? Do you have a prepared response for people's expected displeasure that goes something like, "I'm a Christian, but . . ." or "I'm a member of such and such church, but . . .?" The "church, but" reflex tells us a lot about how we believe we are viewed by the outside culture.

Now contrast what the word "church" means in our culture with what it means in scripture. What are the differences? How did we get here? It is hard to separate the word "church" from all the ways it is used in America. "Church" has lost the sense of being a distinct people with a clear mission in the western world after 1700 years of church being a core institutional presence in our culture. None of that was part of the world of the New Testament. It certainly was not part of Jesus' life and ministry nor those who experienced him.

The early disciples of Jesus didn't really understand the church or the role they were intended to play for a good while, even after the resurrection. It had to unfold as they discovered what God was doing among them as the Spirit led them in an adventure they couldn't pretend to control. "Church" (ecclesia) for them was just a common word for a gathering or assembly of people. It was not a religious word. It had more of a sense of community than organization. It was a relatively empty box that could be filled with meaning for the early believers and it was slow to develop. It included concepts like Kingdom of God, disciple-community (apprentice group), chosen nation, and people of God. All these meanings were rooted in Israel's history. But "church" meant more than any one of these things.

We should not be surprised or alarmed if we have to go through periodic times of confusion about what it means to be the church today. The identity and role of God's people in the world is complicated and breaks all the walls and all the simple boxes where we try to contain it, especially as the world changes around us in dramatic ways. Like everything else, the starting place for deciding what the church is and what it should do needs to be with scripture and not with our current context or cultural heritage.

Before going any farther, we need to read Acts 1:1-11 (NIV):

> In my former book, Theophilus, I wrote about all that
> Jesus began to do and to teach until the day he was taken up to
> heaven, after giving instructions through the Holy Spirit to the
> apostles he had chosen. After his suffering, he presented
> himself to them and gave many convincing proofs that he was
> alive. He appeared to them over a period of forty days and
> spoke about the kingdom of God. On one occasion, while he
> was eating with them, he gave them this command: "Do not
> leave Jerusalem, but wait for the gift my Father promised,
> which you have heard me speak about. For John baptized
> with water, but in a few days you will be baptized with the Holy
> Spirit."
> Then they gathered around him and asked him, "Lord,
> are you at this time going to restore the kingdom to Israel?"
> He said to them: "It is not for you to know the times or
> dates the Father has set by his own authority. But you will
> receive power when the Holy Spirit comes on you; and you will
> be my witnesses in Jerusalem, and in all Judea and Samaria, and
> to the ends of the earth."
> After he said this, he was taken up before their very
> eyes, and a cloud hid him from their sight.
> They were looking intently up into the sky as he was
> going, when suddenly two men dressed in white stood beside
> them. [11] "Men of Galilee," they said, "why do you stand here
> looking into the sky? This same Jesus, who has been taken from
> you into heaven, will come back in the same way you have seen
> him go into heaven."

When Luke says his Gospel (vol. 1 of his two-volume epic) was
about what Jesus "began" to do and teach, he is making a bold claim.
He is saying that Jesus' activity and teaching did not end with the
resurrection of Jesus. Jesus was still doing things and providing
teaching. Acts is the story of what Jesus continues to do through his
Spirit in the people who make up his disciples, community, people, or
church. The church is the continuation of the story of Jesus, which is
the continuation of the story of Israel, which is the continuation of the

story of God, which he launched with the call of Abraham. This is one reason the Book of Acts stops without a conclusion in chapter 28. The story is still ongoing, and God is writing more chapters through his church today. So, it is appropriate that one group of churches today call themselves Acts 29.

Notice what makes up the focus of Jesus' teaching after the resurrection. It is the "Kingdom of God." From what Luke tells us, it's clear that the apostles still did not understand what Jesus was talking about. They are still stuck in an old story about one nation. They think the church is about the liberation, restoration, and glorification of the physical nation of Israel. They are expecting a political hero like Moses or David coming to save and lead them. They are stuck in a national or empire story, but with Israel at the top instead of the bottom this time. They are thinking about war, dominance, and triumph in the modes Israel had known through centuries of contending with empire after empire, from Assyria to Rome.

What Jesus commands them to do is fundamentally different. Instead of calling them to battle and the military rule of other nations, Jesus tells them they will be his witnesses to the ends of the earth. At best, they must have assumed he was talking about proclaiming that Jesus is the Messiah to the Jews scattered around the world and uniting them all in a restored political Israel. Nothing else would have made sense to them yet. Like Peter in Matt. 16, they know Jesus is the Messiah, the "Son of God" (a royal title for them, as in Psalm 2), but they still don't grasp what that means for who they are.

Why was it so hard for the early disciples to understand the international scope of what Jesus was doing? For much the same reason it is hard for us today. We are stuck in other stories that limit our imagination, just like they were.

The early church had phenomenal success in Jerusalem, because of the witness of Jesus, the power of the Spirit, and dramatic witness of the early believers, despite much outright government repression and social opposition. But they didn't grasp what God was doing for a long time. It still seemed like a Jewish story to them. That is why, early on, they stayed in a multi-site, small groups based, mega-church in Jerusalem and only reached out to fellow Jews. In fact, it was hard enough for the early church to deal with cultural tensions among Jewish groups. Going beyond Jews was just unthinkable at this juncture. We turn to that story next in Acts 6:1-7 (NIV):

> In those days when the number of disciples was increasing, the Hellenistic Jews among them complained against the Hebraic Jews because their widows were being overlooked in the daily distribution of food. So the Twelve gathered all the disciples together and said, "It would not be right for us to neglect the ministry of the word of God in order to wait on tables. Brothers and sisters, choose seven men from among you who are known to be full of the Spirit and wisdom. We will turn this responsibility over to them and will give our attention to prayer and the ministry of the word."
> This proposal pleased the whole group. They chose Stephen, a man full of faith and of the Holy Spirit; also Philip, Procorus, Nicanor, Timon, Parmenas, and Nicolas from Antioch, a convert to Judaism. They presented these men to the apostles, who prayed and laid their hands on them.
> 7 So the word of God spread. The number of disciples in Jerusalem increased rapidly, and a large number of priests became obedient to the faith.

It is important to notice that the earliest conflict in the church was cultural—between the Hebraic Jews who kept their distinct traditions of cultural separation and Hellenistic (Greek-speaking) Jews who had adapted to the dominant Greco-Roman culture. This intense Jewish conflict came over into the church and wasn't resolved until the apostles included Hellenistic Jewish leaders in the church. **Any people group in a church who are not represented in leadership will struggle to feel truly accepted**. But, once this cultural barrier was overcome, the church sprinted again. This next stage of rapid growth was led by Phillip and Stephen, a couple of new Hellenistic Jewish leaders. Immediately, they confront the Jewish establishment (cf. Act 7), provoking violent opposition and take the gospel to Ethiopia and Samaria (cf. Acts 8), provoking new controversy.

The expansion of the church/kingdom to include all people groups was deeply problematic and resisted by even the most devoted followers of Jesus. It just didn't fit their expectations or preferences.

They had a long history of separation from the "unclean" nations built into their deepest cultural mindset and codified in their laws. However, they had misunderstood what it meant to be clean, and Jesus had many conflicts about this in his ministry. Despite resistance, Jesus was determined to broaden his people beyond the Jews, and the Spirit continued to break all the boundaries Jesus' early followers set up. The Spirit was leading Jesus' people to embrace a vision of God's people, the church, that was as large as God always intended it to be.

This community of Jesus would be more inclusive than any one community in Judea. It would include the culturally conservative Hebraic Jews and progressive Hellenistic Jews. It would include the Samaritans, who were mixed racially, culturally, and religiously. It would include those excluded by deformity in the Law of Moses. It would even include God-fearing Gentiles who were uncircumcised and outside the bounds of Israel, despite their respect for Israel's God. None of this was going to be easy. Not everyone could accept or advance this mission. But that did not keep the Spirit from leading the church into the fray. The Spirit was not patient about it, nor did the Spirit avoid controversy to get the church to move toward inclusion of all people groups.

In order to reach people outside the normal bounds of Israel, God had to use the people who could be more culturally flexible. It required a Hellenistic Jew like Philip to reach an Ethiopian and Samaritans. Philip was less culturally Jewish, so, therefore, he was more like the Ethiopian and Samaritans. The church expanded from Antioch, which was culturally diverse, more easily than it did from Jerusalem. Yet, this was not easy or peaceful much of the time. The early church was dynamic and controversial. Keeping it together was a constant challenge, which is obvious from Paul's letter more than from The Acts of the Apostles.

Read Acts 8:14-17 (NIV):

When the apostles in Jerusalem heard that Samaria had accepted the word of God, they sent Peter and John to Samaria. When they arrived, they prayed for the new believers there that they might receive the Holy Spirit, because the Holy Spirit had not yet come on any of them; they had simply been baptized in the name of the Lord Jesus. Then Peter and John placed their hands on them, and they received the Holy Spirit.

Notice how the Apostles responded when the gospel first went to Samaritans? They were surprised but willing to accept it. Yet, it still wasn't until great persecution, led by Saul of Tarsus, including the arrest, beatings, and execution of Christians, that the church began to go to Judea, Samaria, and the ends of the earth as Jesus said (cf. Acts 8:1b-3). It seemed to take persecution to get the church moving to the places Jesus sent them in Acts 1:7-8. Why? Likely, because we all naturally connect only with those who are like us. Why go to other countries when there are so many of "our" people who need to know? God would simply not permit this mentality to define his kingdom. He had something bigger in mind.

In Acts 10-11, Peter was not excited about the gospel being open to all people groups. He argued with Jesus. He even told him "No, Lord" when he had a vision of eating unclean food. He resisted going to Simon's house and eating with Gentiles, but he could not deny what the Spirit was calling him to do. The church only accepted God's full mission with reluctance because it broke their definitions of kingdom, nation, or "church." God would not allow the church to serve a mere national agenda. He was restoring an entire world. However, **before we shake our heads and wonder how the Jews and early Christians could be so blind to the larger mission of God, all we have to do is reflect on how we limit Jesus' mission today by conflating it with our national ideologies in stunningly homogenous churches.**

The American church today is much like the Jews of Jesus' day and early Christians in Jerusalem and Judea. We make the same fundamental errors. Israel tended to vacillate between two opposing mistakes through the centuries, both of which damaged their witness, obstructed their mission, and brought about their ruin. These mistakes are still common in the church.

Much of the time, Israel overly assimilated into the broader culture and lost their distinctive identity in a fearful desire to fit in and be respected by the larger culture. They didn't trust the one who called them and saved them to provide, protect, and produce in them what he promised. They thought they had to secure their own safety and blessing by their own wits and skills. This meant making deals with the powers in the world (including the various gods of the nations). They lost their distinctive identity and became just one more nation seeking their own blessing in the world.

Think of Ahab and Jezebel or Manasseh who led Israel to be like the other nations, with an oppressive king culture, trust in military power, worship of other gods, and runaway greed and immorality, even to the point of child-sacrifice. This is what brought about the destruction of Israel and exile.

At other times, Israel tended to retreat into a self-imposed ghetto, where they sat in judgment on "them" (meaning anyone outside their group). They withdrew from the world and rejected and condemned the "nations" from a position of self-righteous arrogance. This is the opposite reaction to the first problem. When Israel embraced their distinctive identity as God's chosen people, they failed to invite the nations into their way of life. They just judged them from a distance.

Think of Jonah or the Pharisees. They wanted the other nations to be destroyed, not saved. Israel often lost their sense of mission and built walls that kept the world out and prayed for God to condemn the world and save them alone. When Israel made this move, they refused to serve the mission of God who called them to model his ways to the world and build roads and bridges for the nations to come near the one true creator God.

Yet, God kept calling Israel to be his agent to reveal himself and extend his reign in all the earth. Jesus came to fulfill that mission and raise up a people who would live out that mission—not as one ethnic group in one location (Jerusalem), but among all people everywhere. In Jesus, God's temple is located in each of us, and collectively as his people we take God's presence wherever we go among the nations.

The church has always had the same two great temptations as Israel. The church has tended to vacillate between being seduced by the world into copying their way of life, or to be appalled by the world— sequestering ourselves in a private enclave that keeps God to ourselves as we wait on him to come destroy the wicked people and vindicate (save) us from the world.

When the church loses either our unique identity, or our sense of mission to model the reign of God, we no longer continue the life and mission of Jesus in the world. We don't cease to exist as

118

a people, but we lose what makes us useful to God and get in the way of his mission. Jesus referred to this as salt without saltiness. It is useless. Either of these moves can destroy our ability to advance God's mission.

Part of the reason these opposing errors have been so common is that they were the strategies employed by the evil one through the principalities and powers of this world. Every ruler (government) among humans throughout time has either opposed the people of God as a threat to be removed or sought to seduce and co-opt the people of God to serve the ruling regime.

If persecution won't drive God's people into a silent submission, seduction usually works just as well or better. While both forms of opposition to God's mission are often at work at some level in all places, we struggle more to recognize and address the ways seduction destroys the church. Persecution is hard to disguise. Not so with seduction. **We are easily taken in by governments who show honor and favor to church leaders and support impressive institutional forms of the church in exchange for loyalty to their regime (and a blind eye to their abuses).**

Sadly, the predominant expression of church in the Western World long ago lost its sense of mission and settled into our world to become a pillar of western culture. We came to see the church as part of Western culture and got seduced into thinking the church was a support for a larger culture or nation instead of an alternative culture within and beyond any state. The mission was outside "our culture" among other nations. This made us blind to the lostness in western cultures and made the church the servant of the state. The decline of the Church in Europe, North America, Australia, New Zealand, and similar areas traces back to corrupt alliances that cost the church its integrity. The churches of western Christendom became an unattractive moral nanny and powerbroker often co-opted by kings, emperors, and the corrupt principalities of our culture. The church backed the kings of the world, supported their supposed divine right to rule and oppress their people, and baptized their holy wars, until the Christian faith, as it had been known, lost credibility with the masses.

The American church has been somewhat of an exception in the decline of the western church, largely because we never had a state church, and entrepreneurial religious leaders have been free to innovate with expressions of church that fit our dynamic and diverse culture. Some of that has been good, but not all of it, by any means. We also shouldn't discount the way God raised up some powerful reform and restoration movements among us that extended the vitality and endurance of the church in our country.

Like the rest of western Christianity, the church in America has also been deeply compromised, politically aligned, and co-opted by the powers of our culture. One symptom of this compromise can be seen in the way White southern churches generally embraced an ideology of manifest destiny, White superiority, and slavery. These churches then logically opposed civil rights as extensions of the "curse of Ham," or refused to address these questions because they were seen as "unspiritual matters" outside the scope of the gospel, which was reduced to address only where people go to heaven after death. There is no calculating the loss of credibility this has cost the church. This is what happens when the church becomes a servant to a culture instead of an alternative to it.

If you ask when the church in the west lived up to some ideal expression of God's intention, you are going to struggle for an answer. The church is only perfected at the end of history, not within it. The church is always broken to some degree and in need of reform, just like all the people who comprise it. Our message is not the church, it is Jesus. As the Apostle Paul said in 2 Corinthians 4:5-7 (NIV):

> For what we preach is not ourselves, but Jesus Christ as Lord, and ourselves as your servants for Jesus' sake. For God, who said, "Let light shine out of darkness," made his light shine in our hearts to give us the light of the knowledge of God's glory displayed in the face of Christ. But we have this treasure in jars of clay to show that this all-surpassing power is from God and not from us.

The way forward is not in looking backward, but in looking ahead to what God is calling us to be and what he will eventually establish when all his work is done.

Despite the pervasive contamination of God's purpose in the churches among us, God is not done with us and continues to call us to

120

more and better forms of Kingdom life. There are encouraging signs of renewal springing up today in a diversity of models, which I'll describe in part in the next chapter. But the forms our faith takes in the future will likely be different than what we have known in the past. There are no sure-fire models to copy. It is time for us to engage in spiritual discernment and holy experimentation. We need some scouts to get out ahead of the wagon train and find some ways forward for the rest of us. Not every trail will work, but we won't be able to navigate the uncharted territory in front of us if we just retrace our steps with more precision.[33]

In my work with Mission Resource Network, we have seen God create rapidly multiplying disciple-making movements of hundreds and at times thousands of small churches who rapidly replicate themselves. We have staff who have been involved with these movements in Rwanda, Burkina Faso, Benin, Cuba, South Africa, and other countries. We have learned from and partnered with leaders who have been a part of similar movements in many other countries on several continents. These churches don't look like the American model and operate among people in different contexts and cultures. However, their existence demonstrates that God's power is still available, and the church is not stuck in western models.[34]

Whatever structures the church takes on, the opportunity is still available for the people of God in the U.S. to recapture our identity and purpose in this generation and be part of a renewal movement that not only impacts our nation but extends throughout our increasing globalized world through our influence. Whatever happens in the USA washes up on the shores of every country. That can be used by God for good if we'll follow him.

Because of his patience and persistence, God has never been without a witness, even in contexts of severe persecution or radically compromised religious institutions. God's Spirit keeps raising up prophets to call his people toward faithfulness, and his Word continues

---

[33] For an explanation of what this entails, I suggest Tod Bolsinger's *Canoeing the Mountains*.

[34] For some description of what this looks like, see *Contagious Disciple-Making* by David and Paul Watson, *The Kingdom Unleashed: How Jesus' 1st-Century Kingdom Values Are Transforming Thousands of Cultures and Awakening His Church*, by Jerry Trousdale and Glenn Sunshine.

to speak and draw his people into the mission that began with Abraham and was fully revealed in Jesus.

Just as the racial and cultural tensions in the early church did not go away quickly or easily, they remain constant challenges for us today. Much of Acts and the epistles deal with Jew versus Gentile issues. And, today, we still battle racial and nationalistic trials. If we are going to follow the Spirit today and be the church Jesus is building, we must let Jesus set the agenda for the church and lead his mission in the world. That sounds good and most Christians would likely say "Amen." But it would serve us well to review the Sermon on the Mount and ask ourselves, "Does this describe the culture and impact of our church?"

The church is a distinct Kingdom: a "nation" in the world comprised of people from every country and culture. Our citizenship is in Jesus' Kingdom, and we live as resident aliens in every country as we confess that he alone is the rightful ruler. That is why we confess that Jesus is both Son of God (identity) and Lord (role). The church should follow and model the ways of the Kingdom as we invite people to join us in the way of the future today. We are a diaspora people without a homeland for now, but who will eventually inherit all the earth when the heavens and earth are restored.

As we reflect on how God called Israel beyond themselves to embrace a vision of being his people for uniting all nations, we need to ask God to reveal to us what people groups we fear, judge, and refuse to love. We need to ask him to give us his heart for them.

Each one of us as individuals and every congregation of God's people need to move into our resistance and develop a plan to engage these people in some form of loving service. We need to find ways to get out of our comfortable church subculture and go outside the church into the communities that scare us. If we do, we'll find that God has already been there developing people who are ready and eager to embrace what God has given us to share.

Putting this into practice

1. Ask God to reveal to you what people you fear, judge, and refuse to love. Ask him to give you his heart for them.

2. Move into your resistance and develop a plan to engage these people in some way in loving service. Find a way to get out of your comfortable church sub-culture and go two-by-two outside the church into a community that scares you.
3. Work with your church, or a few fellow believers to experiment with simple models of churches that meet outside of church buildings in areas where there is a dearth of churches. Contact us at Mission Resource Network if you would like some help imagining what that would look like.

Chapter 12:

Restoring the Church by Rediscovering Our Mission
Getting Back Our Stolen Identity

While the kingdom of God is doing very well world-wide, there is great concern among many Christians in the U.S. about the decline of the institutional expression of church at home. In recent years, we have seen the rise of the "nones" (those who claim no faith), especially among young adults. Almost across the board, churches in the U.S. are seeing declining attendance and membership. Some, like the Churches of Christ of my heritage, are in precipitous decline.[35] Other groups are declining more slowly, but virtually all Christian fellowships that have served the majority White population in the U.S. are in decline.

While the same decline does not seem to be happening among people of color, especially immigrant populations,[36] this does not keep the majority expression of the American church from feeling like it is in trouble. In fact, it is downright scary. Anyone who monitors the activity on social media has seen the increased level of fear and reactivity among Christians. This certainly was a major factor in the presidential elections of 2016 and 2020. The church has begun to lose a sense of social power and with it a privileged place in U.S. culture.[37] The loss of privilege always feels like persecution because we have grown used to power with our sense of entitlement. It is easy to create narratives to justify our status and, once created, those narratives are remarkably resilient, though often just as harmful. It is hard for the

---

[35] "A Case Study of Growth and Decline: The Churches of Christ, 2006-2016," by Stanley E. Granberg, *Great Commission Research Journal*, Vol. 10, No. 1, Fall 2018, pp. 88-110.

[36] Soong-Chan Rah, *The Next Evangelicalism: Freeing the Church from Western Cultural Captivity,* esp. pp. 13-14, 169-70.

[37] This is different from "White privilege" in the way that I'm discussing it here, but the two do overlap.

majority White church in the USA to read books like 1 Peter or Hebrews and make sense of all the talk of being exiles, aliens, and oppressed. Though we manage to feel persecuted when we do lose any privilege.

While there are many sociological explanations for why this might be happening, especially with reference to some Christian groups in particular, there are some deeper causes which are impacting all believers in Jesus addressed throughout this work. In short, the church in the U.S., along with much of the West, is in trouble because we lost our sense of mission. The church allowed itself to be domesticated by the larger culture and we lost our unique identity, role, and purpose. While some structural or programmatic changes may help a few churches grow, often by cannibalizing other congregations, these churches will likely be the exceptions unless there are more sweeping changes among believers in Jesus. What we really need is a restoration of the church's core self-understanding and purpose in the world.

When we read passages like Acts 20:1-7, Philemon 1-2, or Ephesians 4:1-6, 11-16, it is obvious that the dynamic church we read about in the New Testament looked very different from what we know today. The early church was not an institution with set forms, roles, rituals, and programs. It was a loose network of people who shared a unique self-understanding, purpose, and collective identity over against the Roman Empire and local nations it dominated. The church was a people movement with minimal forms and nothing approaching institutional expression.

The earliest churches met where they could find space, usually in the homes of members wealthy enough to have a house that could hold a sizable group. While there was some sense of order to events, built around customs picked up from the synagogue and other groups from the local cultures, the gatherings appeared to be flexible meetings built around a common meal or Lord's Supper, stories and teachings from Jesus and the apostles, and the needs of the group at the time. Paul's instructions in 1 Corinthians 12 and 14 make it clear that these gatherings could get chaotic, at least in the Gentile dominated areas, and they were not always productive. But we can also see a dynamism and freedom in them that is typically missing in the tightly programmed American churches of our day.

The early church met in the evenings, because the first day of the week was not a day off in any culture of that era. Since the church met in scattered homes, they did not operate in ways that we take for granted. They were one church with a common identity but that identity was not rooted in meeting locations, programs, events, or staff. They could be a single "church" in a city while meeting in multiple locations. They didn't worry about such things as programs, branding, or staff, but they did have ministry, identity, and leadership. The church grew fastest in the first three centuries before it was legal, could own property, or institutionalize in any meaningful way. That should say something to us. While institutional structures, formal leader training, and events with high production value may be helpful for churches at times, and are not wrong per se, they can't replace the dynamic power of a grassroots people movement with a clear mission.

In the past century, the fastest growth of the kingdom of God has been in China. In 1948, when the Maoist communist party took over China, they drove the church underground and removed its entire institutional presence; there were fewer than 3 million Christians, mainly in western-looking churches, planted by leaders from Europe and the USA. During the revolution and communist takeover, all churches and seminaries were closed, their property confiscated, and all the church leaders imprisoned unless they bowed to the state and limited their activity to the government-controlled church. The faithful church went underground, meeting in secret small groups with nothing but their faith, their Bibles, and the Spirit – and the church silently exploded. Today, there are estimated to be in excess of 100 million Christians in China.[38] Some estimate there may be as many as 130 million Jesus followers in China.[39] We can learn from what God has done in China. **The power of the church is not found in its institutional presence, but in its purpose and submission to God.**

---

[38] Paul Borthwick, *Western Christians in Global Mission: What's the Role of the North American Church?*, p. 36. Mark Noll, *The New Shape of World Christianity: How American Experience Reflects Global Faith*, pp. 20-21.

[39] "China's Christians keep the faith, rattling the country's leaders" in The Nikkei Asian Review, TSUKASA HADANO, September 10, 2019. https://asia.nikkei.com/Politics/China-s-Christians-keep-the-faith-rattling-the-country-s-leaders.

I know of a disciple-making movement in Cuba that has over 14,000 churches and is growing rapidly. But they are not counted on any official register of the government or any institutional churches. They are not part of any denomination or recognized religious tradition. They don't exist formally and yet they are transforming the places where they are. They are vulnerable yet dynamic. The future of the church will likely come from places like this. We won't think or plan our way into a brighter future. Only God can lead that. But we can cultivate the posture of humility, spiritual discernment, mindset and practices to follow what God is doing as we recover our sense of mission.

We may be tempted to ask if we are the same church we read about in the New Testament if we don't reproduce the same forms of the early church. But we need to beware of confusing forms with identity. We don't have to copy forms to be the same people with the same mission.

The synagogue was never mentioned in the OT. It was an innovation of a people who lived in exile without the temple or priesthood of the past. Yet, the synagogue played a critical role in preserving the faith and identity of Israel. This is a perfect example of new forms arising to serve new times and needs. Jesus and the apostles made good use of the synagogue to serve God's mission. Jesus was critical of the temple and priestly system, which were prescribed in scripture, because they no longer served God's purpose in his day. **Purpose matters more than structure**.

It would be foolish to reject all attempts to gather the church into larger institutional expressions. This seems to be an inevitable outcome as the church gains traction and size in any culture. As the church grows among a people group, it must address the needs of people to learn how to live out their faith in their culture. This becomes increasingly complex over the generations. It is natural and helpful for the church to begin to organize and develop standard, efficient ways to meet those needs. But, as the church organizes and centralizes, it also easily turns inward and loses a passion for its mission to reach "the nations." We need to keep a focus on expanding the boundaries of the kingdom even as we seek to solidify the gains and make sure we serve well those who have become part of the Jesus movement.[40]

Our mission is not to build great congregations, or even to draw people from every community into our church, as admirable as those goals may be. They can be part of advancing our mission. However, our primary mission is to get Christ and his life into all the people and communities in our city, region, nation, and the world. It is about restoring all that has been broken by the rejection of God's rightful reign. If our congregation is accomplishing this purpose well, it is a good thing and we should seek to preserve it. If our congregation is not producing this kind of fruit, it needs to be re-evaluated and retooled or re-tasked to serve God's purpose in the world.

If Jesus were to speak to a convention of American church leaders today, I think he would say, "If you seek to save your church, you will lose it. But, if you will lose your church for my sake and the gospel, you will find it again." We need to be willing to put the institutional church we've known at risk for the sake of the kingdom. Seeking to preserve the models of church we have may distract us from doing what would make the gospel vibrant and impactful in our day.

While large institutional churches, which make us feel powerful and relevant in this world, can also serve as useful tools in God's hands, they are not the norm for the faithful people of God through the ages. They can also distract us from our larger purpose when they turn inward and become obsessed with their own survival, or even worse, their social power. When a congregation becomes the end instead of the means, it has fallen away from God's primary mission and has begun moving toward idolatry, irrelevancy, corruption, and obstruction of God's mission. We need to get the purpose of the local congregation clear so that it can advance the mission for which God created the people he calls "The Church."

The large institutional form of the church we have known in the U.S., with expansive facilities for worship, Bible classes, and suites of offices for large professional ministerial staffs, is a luxury. It is not wrong, and God can certainly use it powerfully when it is healthy, but it is fraught with dangers. In such a powerful expression, the mission of

---

[40] I am indebted to John King of Final Command ministries for the language I borrow here.

the church can be removed from the people and laid at the feet of the professionals that the people merely support financially as they attend events and receive services. Most people in the churches who operate from this model have become consumers of the mission instead of the mission's workforce. When the church is turned into a passive consumer of religious goods and services provided by a paid professional staff, the mission has almost disappeared. Too often the church loses its mission as it centralizes. What was intended to strengthen the church ends up merely enabling it to become passive.

This process is normal and understandable, but it is still lethal. It typically develops later in the process of the gospel's acceptance within a culture as the church shifts from being a fringe people movement to an established part of a culture.[41] The church, properly understood as the people of God, will of necessity take on many forms as it emerges and develops over time among various cultures and countries. The development of Christian faith in a culture tends to follow a predictable pattern that flows from dynamic people movement to formalizing and eventually to declining, entrenched institutions. Hopefully, as this sets in, the church goes back through revival and reform as God works among us. This was the pattern of Israel and it has been the pattern of the church.

Israel started as a single family, and then became a loose collection of tribes with a common ancestry and language but no homeland or structure. They then became a more formalized nation on the move with God through the wilderness without land, but with an increasingly clear identity and structures (leadership, religious institutions and practices). They worshiped in a tent and were a mobile people that drew in foreigners who wanted to be connected to their God. In time, God gave them a land and they became a loose network of tribes without centralized leadership for several centuries. Eventually, they wanted and got a king, built a permanent temple, and increasingly put their trust in their institutions (monarchy; a standing army; institutional religions with priests, rituals, and a temple; and expanding bureaucracy, rooted in institutions).

---

[41] "4 Stages of a Movement" by Steve Smith, Neill Mims, and Mark Steves (Mission Frontiers, Nov/Dec, 2015).

While this was acceptable, and even good for a while, eventually Israel lost their trust in the God who delivered them and provided for them in the wilderness, and concluded they had to secure their own future by their own wisdom and institutions. They cut deals with other nations, copying their ways, and corruption set in. God shook them out of their calcified self-serving ways by allowing a series of tragedies and military defeats, which produced temporary reforms, but never produced lasting change. They fragmented and became increasingly corrupt until eventually, God allowed both the northern and southern kingdoms to be defeated, and the people scattered among the nations.

Then, once again in exile, stripped of formal structures and institutions, Israel became a people group with a compelling story rooted in God's story, even though they were no longer an established nation-state. In exile they had no king, no temple, and no functioning priesthood. They had only prophets and scripture and a faith in God. Once again, in a second exodus story (from Babylon instead of Egypt this time) God acted in history to save them and they became a people on the move who started the process over with a similar cycle and nearly identical outcome.

When Israel was a people with a dynamic faith on mission, they were spiritually strong and vital, though they looked structurally vulnerable. The more they centralized their power and became institutional, the quicker they trusted themselves and moved toward eventual decline. It didn't happen quickly, but it happened repeatedly.

The Gospels all make the case that national Israel was not the full story of God. Jesus was the next and climactic episode in the story of God which transcends any nation or institution. Jesus is the fulfillment of all the hopes, dreams, purposes, prophecies, and work of God's people from that day on. Jesus fully embodied Israel and her purpose. He is the ultimate prophet who calls for repentance and return to God, casts a vision for what God is doing in the world, and leads God's people to restoration and refocus on our identity and purpose.

Jesus is the final High Priest, sacrifice, and temple that removes our sin, unites us to God, and represents the presence of God among his people. He is the Anointed King (known as Messiah among the Jews) who came to unite and reconstitute the people of God. He expands God's holy people to include all nations and all realms of the earth. He is God, come to live among those made in God's image, so the intended intimacy between God and humanity can be restored and the creation can become what it was intended to be from before creation.

Jesus takes on the entire purpose and life of Israel, brings it to new depths, reveals the extent of what he has been doing, and raises up a multi-ethnic community who take his life and mission into all the world as he works through them to fulfill God's mission until all is set right, by his empowering Spirit.

This is the purpose of God's people who follow Jesus. Like Israel of old, the dominant expressions of the American church are sliding into the same kind of post-Christian malaise of the other countries of the former western Christendom. This decline may resolve itself in reform and revival, or it may move toward irrelevance and dissolution. Regardless, we will not get out of this condition by doing the same things we have always done even bigger and better. Tactical tweaks won't get us through this cultural change, even if they feel huge to disoriented long-time church members. A new style of worship and better programming will not be enough. God is at work around the world and within the U.S. in new and fresh ways. **We must get back to our calling, identity, and mission and move into vulnerability to find vitality**. Our goal should not be to save our institutional churches, per se, but to serve the mission of God with all the resources he has put at our disposal.

This is not a call for churches to disband as irrelevant. Rather, it is a call to restore our idea, role, and mission in the world even if it puts our existing churches at risk. For some churches, a move into mission will likely extend their vitality and lead to growth in number and spirit. For others, it may require reinvesting in new forms of church that will outlive and outgrow the current model as it moves into a blessed sacrifice of its life for the sake of the Kingdom. **The future of the church does not rest in the perpetuation of our current congregations but in the extension of Jesus' life in our world through us, in whatever forms that takes.**

I have seen many church models spring up around the U.S. with varying degrees of impact. Some are small groups meeting in homes, apartments, or coffee shops. Some even meet in empty bars on Sunday mornings and set up and tear down every time they meet. Some meet in bowling alleys, restaurants, hotel conference rooms, and countless other meeting places. Some, like Mosaic in Little Rock, meet in renovated old shopping centers and lease space to people-serving organizations to help people in need in their neighborhoods. Models are easy to come by and none is foolproof. Most models can succeed or fail depending on leadership, timing, context, and intangible factors we'll never understand. Models are not what make things work. God works, people work, vision and mission work, but models can only facilitate or obstruct things. Americans have an addiction to models when we need to be addicted to mission.

Where there is a vision, passion, and spiritual life, forms will typically follow. But great models run by good leaders with "best practices" can still fail gloriously. Most new churches don't live long, and that isn't all bad. Failing in the right direction in a way that gives life can be a Kingdom win. Succeeding in the wrong direction in a way that incarnates the wrong values and mission is a kingdom fail. Our goal isn't to build enduring institutions, but to expand the reign of God over the lives of people and be agents of redemption and restoration. **What hurts the American church is not our lack of good models so much as our lost sense of mission.**

The greatest distraction in the American church today is likely American Nationalism, which seeks to make the church a tool to prop up the USA as a nation-state and conflates patriotism with devotion to God. The narrative of America as an exceptional Christian nation is a naïve distortion driven by questionable motives. It is at best a distraction and at worst a form of idolatry. The Kingdom of God is not an American story, though casting it that way can be irresistibly tantalizing.

If you ask at what point America was a paragon of Christian virtue, you won't get any good answers. Was it during the era of slavery? Was it during the era of Jim Crow? Was it during the era of psychedelic drug experimentation and sexual revolution? Of course not, but those were all part of American culture in "the good old days." While not everything in our past is bad, and there is much to commend, there is no time in American history when the church got it right. There is no ideal past we just need to recapture. That is based on nostalgia, which is the glorification of an idealized past that never existed. Rather, Jesus calls us to move forward toward the vision God has always had for his people which has never been fully realized in this world.

As hard as it is for many of us to face, America has always fallen way short of being a Christian nation and was established as an intentionally secular state where all religions could operate without interference from the state. However, at that time, the religions present were overwhelmingly variations of Christianity, and the general culture was deeply influenced by Christian faith, making America seem more Christian than it was set up to be formally.[42] Today's religious pluralism is much more difficult to navigate, and it is unclear whether any nation can be truly united with the level of diversity we are experiencing. That scares me as an American who loves my country. But, as a follower of Jesus, I need to be reminded that the church is not ultimately invested in national security. It is commissioned to serve God's Kingdom. There have been plenty of times when the kingdom has advanced best with nations that were collapsing.

The ministry I work for has been working with Muslim background believers around the Mediterranean Sea. Most are refugees from four countries in the Middle East: Syria, Iraq, Iran, and Afghanistan. I have been astonished by how many people from these lands have told us not to pray for peace in their country, because it is the instability that is opening people to Jesus. That is hard to hear and hard to do when you see the suffering that comes to those who are fleeing, but from a Kingdom perspective, it is not that hard to understand.

Our hope is not in America but the Kingdom of God. Patriotism (love of our homeland) is a good and healthy thing for every people group, if it is recognized to be a lower value than love of God and his Kingdom. But nationalism, the belief that our nation is God's favorite people and the church is a pillar to support our exceptional nation, is a form of idolatry. Both sides of the political spectrum in our nation are constantly seeking to co-opt the church for their idealized visions of America's future, because this is what the principalities and powers of

---

[42] For more on this subject, see *Myths America Lives*, Richard Hughes.

134

the world always do. Kingdom people will recognize and decline to subordinate the gospel to any national agenda.

We have a bigger vision, an alternative vision to that of any nation, which makes us odd and often misunderstood in our culture when we live it out. Disciples of Jesus will see the need to interact with the larger social and political forces of our day in diverse ways. And we need people who love Jesus to engage every group in our culture, including the political parties. But we need to beware of confusing Kingdom of God work and restoring-the-power-of-America-as-a-nation work. No political group on the left or right defines greatness for us. Only God can do that for his people.

If the church is living out our mission, the powers of this world will struggle to understand us and will seek to seduce us or oppose us. They always have. That is the norm for us and shouldn't surprise or bewilder us. America will respond to Jesus in the same ways the nation of Israel did. Some will join; others will oppose. The Kingdom of God was not about saving the nation of Israel but about drawing Israel and all nations into the larger vision and life of God's Kingdom. The same is true of the Kingdom of God and any nation today, including the USA.

Being a compassionate and just nation is not the full mission of God, as good as it is. We are God's tool to effect change beyond ourselves. A similar but less dangerous distraction to conservative churches in the U.S. is the move toward being a "relevant" social services institution that abandons our distinct identity as God's people and simply seeks to do good and bless people without calling them to repentance and new life in Jesus. This is an attempt to win the admiration of the larger culture through our compassion without drawing the criticism of the larger culture by speaking up about hard truths and calling for people to surrender their worldviews and values to the Kingdom of Jesus.

Following Jesus will simultaneously make us better citizens and subversive aliens in every country. We must live in the continual tension of being in, but not of, the world—in, but not of, every nation. We are called to be respectful citizens who pray for our leaders and work for the good of our nation, while being prophetic voices who are not afraid to address uncomfortable truths in the church and in the public square.[43] The church is called to respect our rulers and challenge their idolatrous abuses of power and constant efforts to make all people bow to the principalities and powers that inhabit every regime and nation state. Without taking up the sword or using power as governments do, we must resist the constant seduction of the culture and the powers of every nation's leadership who may give up on directly opposing us and try to co-opt us instead.

The greatest hope for the church in America is to give up trying to save our churches or nation and to invest completely in serving the mission of God and extending his reign in the world. We are called to make disciples and form self-replicating holistic Kingdom communities among all people groups. Jesus' words speak to us, "You must give up your life to find it." We need to put our churches at risk to serve the larger purpose of God. For some churches this will lead to renewal and growth (with great travail). For others, it will mean the death of the institution, but the expansion of the Kingdom.

The goal is not the preservation of any one congregation, but the expansion of God's reign through Jesus as he increases his territory through more and more lives, neighborhoods, and people groups. The way up is to step down. The way to find life is to embrace our death while trusting God's power to raise those who obey him. Jesus calls us to sacrifice our life to find it. **The question is: which do we love more, God and his mission, or our churches that serve "us" well?**

No one congregation can reach all people. We need multiple congregations working together in Kingdom fellowship but serving in many neighborhoods to see that the Kingdom goes to all people in ways that fit them. The era of the large, big-tent church that serves all people is likely waning as God is raising up dynamic people movements and networks of diverse models of Kingdom communities. Big churches are great, and we need them. The more the better, if they are healthy. But they are expensive and adapt slowly. Nothing fails quite like organizations that are "too big to fail." They invariably end up sacrificing people to preserve their platform. They just can't meet all the needs of our mission or serve all people.

---

[43]Cf., the contrast between Romans 13:1-7 and Revelation – i.e., chapters 17-18 – and how they view Rome and counsel Christians to engage their government.

Churches in the U.S. badly need to rediscover how to keep score and determine what is a win in God's economy. While every church should be reaching out and drawing in people, not everyone we can reach for Jesus will fit in our existing congregations. We need more than one way to serve the Kingdom than through church growth. The ultimate goal is not to get more people in our churches but to get Christ in more people.

The problems come in when the institutions we create become more important than the people who comprise them, and when the church is reduced to an institution that serves itself instead of a people with a mission in the world. How can we make the model of church we have work at its best for those who are well served by this model, while at the same time joining God's Spirit in starting new communities of faith who can reach people who will not come to what we have here?

We need both-and strategies instead of either-or strategies. We want to see our churches grow and start new groups who can become churches to reach more people. Our existing churches play a critical role in the mission, but the mission is not to save our present churches. Churches cannot be saved; only people can.

Putting this into practice

1. Pray about starting a new church in your neighborhood. It could be an institutional church or just a small house church. There are numerous ministries available to help you get started and coach you in their models.
2. Ask your church leadership where church planting fits in their vision. Become an advocate for new church planting and experimenting and various models.
3. Don't wait on the institutional church to lead. You can start small and do things with just a handful of people. Don't worry about failing. Worry about getting stuck in a way of doing church that has proven it is not going to be relevant into the future.

Appendix:

Additional Resources Suggested

- *The Mission of God: Unlocking the Bible's Grand Narrative* by Christopher JH Wright
- *The Gospel in a Pluralist Society* by Lesslie Newbigin
- *Theological Worlds: Understanding the Alternative Rhythms of Christian Belief* by W. Paul Jones
- *The 3D Gospel: Ministry in Guilt, Shame, and Fear Cultures* by Jayson Georges
- *Missionary Methods: St. Paul's or Ours* by Roland Allen
- *Renovation of the Heart* by Dallas Willard
- *Surprised by Hope* by NT Wright
- *The Next Evangelicalism* by Soong-Chan Rah
- *Learning to Listen, Learning to Teach* by Jane Vella

Dan Bouchelle – Author

Dan has served as the president of MRN since August 2010.

Before taking the lead of this international missions ministry, Dan served in congregational ministry for over two decades with three different churches in Texas and Oklahoma. He also served on the boards of Great Cities Missions and Christian Relief Fund, as well as other community service and para-church boards.

Dan has worked with churches on six continents and congregations throughout the US. He has also spoken at colleges, lectureships, workshops, and seminars around the globe. He has published several articles and has written three books: *The Gospel Unleashed*, *The Gospel Unhindered*, and *When God Seems Absent*.

In preparation for ministry, Dan acquired a BS in Psychology from the University of Houston—Clear Lake, an MA, MDiv, and DMin from Abilene Christian University.

Dan married his wife Amy in 1987 and God blessed them with three children: Anna and Seth, who are both grown, and Abby who still lives at home. They are proud grandparents of two.

Who We Are
HCU Media LLC

Publishing in support of

Heritage Christian University – Ghana (HCU Ghana)

www.hcuc.edu.gh

HCU media has been established to support the publication of materials, both paper and electronic, created by faculty and friends of HCU Ghana. These materials will be offered initially in the USA & Ghana but may become available globally via other outlets.